AMERICAN ETCHER

A·B·R·O·A·D

1880 ✤ 1939

AMERICAN ETCHERS
A·B·R·O·A·D
1880 ❦ 1939

By Reed Anderson

Spencer Museum of Art
The University of Kansas

American Etchers Abroad, 1880-1939
Exhibition organized by Reed Anderson, Ph.D. candidate at
The University of Kansas, Kress Foundation Department of Art History, for
the Spencer Museum of Art, Lawrence, Kansas, April 3 – June 6, 2004.

This catalogue is made possible through the generous support of the
Marilyn J. Stokstad Publications Fund.

This catalogue accompanies the exhibition of the same name at
the Spencer Museum of Art, The University of Kansas.

Front Cover Image:
John Taylor Arms
United States, 1887-1953
Somewhere in France, 1919
Etching on laid paper
308 x 152 mm
12 1/8 x 6 inches
Spencer Museum of Art, The University
of Kansas: Anonymous gift, 1998.182

Back Cover Image:
James Abbott McNeill Whistler
United States, 1834-1903
The Unsafe Tenement, 1858
Etching on laid paper
157 x 224 mm
6 3/16 x 8 7/8 inches
Spencer Museum of Art, The University
of Kansas: Gift of John J. Talleur and Ann
Talleur Collection, 1991.270

Title Image:
Frank Duveneck
United States, 1848-1919
The Rialto, 1883
Etching on Whatman paper
286 x 475 mm
11 1/4 x 18 7/8 inches
Spencer Museum of Art, The University
of Kansas: Museum purchase, 2003.108

Edited by Bill Woodard
Photography by Robert Hickerson
Designed by Austin Porter
Printed at James Printing, Kansas City, Missouri
Text: Minion, Minion Italic, Minion Bold

C O N T E N T S

To my Mother, with much love and thanks.

ACKNOWLEDGMENTS

Many creative minds and talents have contributed to the success of *American Etchers Abroad, 1880-1939*. For her early and sustained interest and guidance I thank Dr. Andrea Norris, former Director, Spencer Museum of Art. Not only did Dr. Norris guide me through the labyrinth of organizing an exhibition, she also contributed valuable editorial assistance on the catalogue. Special thanks are also due Dr. Stephen Goddard, Curator of Prints and Drawings, Spencer Museum of Art, whose passion for prints and printmaking is genuine and infectious. In addition to lending scholarly advice, Dr. Goddard also provided moral support on the few occasions when the task at hand, compounded by other responsibilities, seemed especially overwhelming, as did Dr. Marilyn Stokstad, Professor Emerita, Kress Foundation Department of Art History, University of Kansas, who kindly supported the publication of the catalogue with a generous financial contribution.

The Spencer Museum of Art is blessed with an incredible staff, many of whom are deserving of special recognition. The organizational skills of Assistant Director Carolyn Chinn Lewis ensured that the project ran smoothly. The catalogue's talented designer Austin Porter and editor Bill Woodard were uncommonly receptive to my endless requests to make last-minute revisions. The exquisite reproductions are due to the high standards of Robert Hickerson, the museum's photographer, and his assistant Kate Meyer. I thank all of them for producing a catalogue that has surpassed all expectations. Janet Dreiling, Registrar, and Richard Klocke, Exhibition Designer, contributed their expertise to the exhibition.

James and Virginia Moffett and Joel Dryer graciously loaned important works, which allowed me to cast a wider net and include other deserving etchers in the exhibition. I extend heartfelt thanks to John R. Poindexter, Ph. D., for sharing with me his knowledge of Herman Armour Webster and Donald Shaw MacLaughlan; and to the latter's grand-niece Linda Harrington, for answering many questions about her fascinating uncle. I look forward to working with both of them in the years ahead on future projects. Last but not least, I must thank Robert Hileman, who read the text in its early stages and offered many helpful comments and suggestions.

Reed Anderson

PREFACE

American Etchers Abroad, 1880-1939 first came to my attention in my graduate museum training class in fall 2002, when Reed Anderson presented the project for a class assignment to conceive an exhibition and write a proposal for it. His was such a good project—so clearly articulated, carefully defined, and something that would make a specific contribution to scholarship—that I wished we could do the exhibition at the Spencer. So it was a complete delight when I discovered that Reed thought of the exhibition as a real project and that he and curator of prints and drawings Steve Goddard had been discussing it for some time.

Shortly thereafter, Steve Goddard let me know that Marilyn Stokstad was interested in supporting the project with an endowment she had recently established at the Kansas University Endowment Association, dedicated to supporting publications from the KU Libraries and the Spencer Museum of Art. The fund supports only Spencer publications that document and publish research on the permanent collection. Since Reed's exhibition is primarily drawn from the Spencer's own collection of American prints, it was ideally qualified for the Stokstad funding. With a few revisions, we sent his proposal from class to Professor Stokstad and the Endowment Association, where it was enthusiastically received. Thanks go to Marilyn Stokstad and the KUEA for supporting important graduate student research on significant and inadequately recognized parts of the Spencer Museum's collection.

This exhibition could not have been organized at the Spencer fifteen years ago, because the museum did not have its current depth of collections in American prints. In 1998 the Spencer received the gift of an extensive and rich collection of American and Japanese prints from a generous donor who still wishes to remain anonymous. The gift created exceptional strengths in the print collection in areas that had previously been quite thin—particularly late nineteenth- and early twentieth-century American prints—exactly the period of *American Etchers Abroad, 1880-1939.* With this publication the museum can take advantage of these new holdings in order to present new findings on a group of artists who participated in the American etching revival and who also were among the large group of expatriate artists who studied, painted, and etched in Italy, Germany, Britain and France at the end of the nineteenth and the beginning of the twentieth century.

I am proud to have been involved in the organization of this exhibition, which brings attention to works of art of importance and interest that have often been overlooked, which documents part of a rich and broad print collection, and which enables a young and committed scholar to present his research in this attractive exhibition and catalogue.

Andrea S. Norris, Ph.D.
former Director

F. O. Marvin
United States, 1852-1915
The Old Mill of Lawrence, ca. 1885
Etching
Spencer Museum of Art,
The University of Kansas:
Gift of Mrs. C.L. Burt, 1973.100

FOREWORD

When, shortly before 1900, the Belgian artist James Ensor (1860-1949) referred to the "delicious work of the etcher," he was expressing a fondness for a way of making prints that was enjoying an international vogue that would continue well into the twentieth century. From its first applications as a printmaking medium around 1500 to the work of contemporary printmakers, the singular characteristics of etching have offered a seductive array of technical and aesthetic possibilities that distinguish it from other printmaking processes. In addition to the allure to participate in an illustrious tradition established by earlier practitioners such as Callot, Rembrandt, and Goya, etching allows the artist to make marks in a manner that approximates drawing, it is capable of extremely fine linear details or broad, wash-like effects, and the actual act of printing the etched plate offers many possibilities for a large variety of nuanced effects. Polished copper etching plates, sharp needles and smooth burnishers, recipes and acids also appeal to artists who like to indulge in what a current student has aptly characterized as printmaking's penchant for magical effects.[1]

Within the scope of the international enthusiasm for etching—commonly dubbed, "the etching revival"—the work of American artists offers a rich and complex chapter, and within that chapter the story of works by artists who chose to combine foreign travel and etching is especially fascinating. A sense of the broad sweep of the etching revival in America can be gleaned from the activities of artists working at the geographical center of the country, where the current exhibition was realized. To appreciate the extent of America's fascination with etching one need only imagine the sign that is reported to have announced "Seeds & Etchings" over the door of James Smalley and Company's seed and feed store in McPherson, Kansas.[2] Whether or not this sign existed, it is certain that James Smalley's son, Carl (1885-1965), who was to become one of the state's most ambitious and dedicated promoters of art, ran a fledgling art shop in the family store before 1920.

A key figure in Lawrence, Kansas, was F. O. Marvin (1852-1915), professor (and later dean) of engineering at the University of Kansas. He is important not so much for the many capable landscape plates that he etched as for the clear record he left as a fully informed participant in the etching revival. He used a variety of inks and papers with great sensitivity, he collected the works of the etchers who were championed in the literature of the day, and his personal library included many of the books that Reed Anderson emphasizes in his essay in this volume, including those by Sylvester Rosa Koehler and Philip Gilbert Hamerton.[3] Though it is not certain that Marvin ever made his way to Europe, other Kansas etchers did, including Mary Huntoon (1896-1970) of Topeka, who studied etching with Joseph Pennell (1857-1926) in Philadelphia, and Arthur W. Hall (1889-1981, active in Kansas from 1923-1942) who studied with the etcher E.S. Lumsden (1883-1948) in Scotland.

If the microcosm of one land-locked state can boast participation in the interna-

[1] Kelly J. Clark, in his paper for my class, *History of Prints*, "Magic Medium: Artistic Trickery in the Printmaking Process," Fall 2003.

[2] Bill North, "Prairie Impressions: The Prairie Print Makers and Print Culture in Kansas," in *The Prairie Print Makers* (Kansas City, Mo.: Exhibits USA, Mid-America Arts Alliance, 2001), 20-26.

[3] I am grateful to Edward Barr, whose 1995 paper for Professor Charles Eldredge's American Art class, "Frank O. Marvin: Kansas Printmaker," provides an excellent overview.

tional phenomenon of the etching revival, then it will be no surprise that the full account of American etchers abroad promises a great deal for any student of the history of American art, especially when the story is told by as insightful an enthusiast as Reed Anderson. It is always gratifying when a student's interests and abilities align with material that begs for re-examination. Happily this has been the case in the current exhibition and catalogue, which represent a confluence of recent donations of artwork and support to the museum and the arrival in our graduate program of someone perfectly matched to the task of undertaking this project. I am grateful to have worked with and mentored Reed Anderson during his yearlong internship and I am delighted that the generous support of Marilyn Stokstad has made this volume possible.

—Stephen H. Goddard
Curator of Prints and Drawings

A MERICAN E TCHERS A BROAD , 1 8 8 0 - 1 9 3 9

"Travel is fatal to prejudice, bigotry, and narrow-mindedness..."

- Mark Twain

The Innocents Abroad, 1869

The closing decades of the nineteenth century witnessed a significant number of American painters traveling abroad, some of them surely inspired by Mark Twain's witty and immensely popular, no-nonsense guide to Europe and the Holy Land. Swayed by the increasing popularity of etching in America and elsewhere, many of these painters put aside their paint pots and brushes in order to register their impressions of Europe and the Orient on the copper plate.[1] Essentially self-taught in the art of etching, they were given an exceptional amount of freedom in developing their individual styles. Yet collectively, they shared a romantic sensibility, as was demonstrated by their predilection to represent things as they once were and will never be again. With lightened baggage, they scoured the earth in search of the picturesque and the exotic, which some of them discovered in the medieval streets and courtyards of Paris, the slumbering canals of Venice, and the congested marketplaces of Cairo and Constantinople. Their curiosities satisfied, many returned home and settled back into a comfortable life in the United States, content with their souvenirs and remembrances. However, a few chose to remain abroad, establishing their reputations in their adopted countries. By the end of the century, this mass migration to foreign shores had ebbed significantly, only to be reborn in the early decades of the twentieth century, when another wave of American painters ventured abroad, many of them treading in the footsteps of their predecessors.

❦

The grand tour that Twain and others embarked upon was, in many ways, *de rigueur* for American artists, who had been traveling to Europe and the Orient for generations to immerse themselves in art's rich and glorious history. They received inspiration and instruction from the works of the Old Masters hanging in the galleries of the Louvre, the Uffizi, and the Prado, as well as the great architectural monuments they encountered during their travels, such as the Colosseum in Rome, St. Martin's Bridge in Toledo, and the magnificent Cathedral of Chartres. American etchers had chosen to go abroad for several generations also, and for similar reasons. George Loring Brown (1814-89) and John Gadsby Chapman (1808-89) were among the first, and although they are today best known for their paintings, both men were also accomplished etchers. Importantly, they created many original etchings while

[1] Although terms like "The Orient" and "exotic" have come to denote a Eurocentric world view and thus taken on pejorative connotations in recent years, they were in vogue during the period under consideration and have been retained here for that reason.

living and working in Italy, the majority of these based on actual sites and tinted with their idyllic sentiments.

Chapman, author of the popular and enduring *American Drawing Book: A Manual for the Amateur and Basis of Study for the Professional Artist* (1847), is the first notable figure in American illustration. He was a prolific etcher, as demonstrated by the fourteen hundred illustrations he created for *Harper's Family Bible* (1846). Chapman fell under Italy's spell during his first trip abroad, a three-year excursion that began in 1828. He returned in 1848 and remained until 1884, his studio in Rome becoming a major destination for many American artists who were then studying in Europe. Chapman spoke for many of his generation who chose to live and work abroad when he wrote, "In Rome I have every reason to be happy and contented. In a professional point of view I have all that I could desire, facilities of study and production, profitable association with art and artists of every nation at all times, and...I am free from the wearing toil I formerly endured in New York."[2] Some of the artists associated with the etching revival were of a like mind, such as Julius Rolshoven and A. C. Webb, who also chose to live as expatriates.

While residing in Rome, Chapman needled many romantic landscapes of the Italian countryside on the copper plate, such as *Prato Lungo*, 1850-60, in which picturesque ruins, an old stone bridge spanning a quiet stream, and an ox-driven wagon suggest an ancient way of life drawing to a close. It has been suggested that Chapman produced these prints for the tourist trade since they never appeared as illustrations in any publication.[3] In addition to prints like *Prato Lungo*, which he may have sold individually, Chapman produced a portfolio composed of four etchings and titled *Italian Life and Scenery*, which he advertised in *The Crayon* from March 21 to June 27, 1855. Despite the lengthy notice, the etchings failed to attract buyers.

George Loring Brown lived in Rome from 1840 to 1859, and although undocumented, it is possible that he and Chapman met each other; the strong similarities in their etchings suggest that Brown was at least aware of Chapman's work. Enchanted by the Italian way of life, he too established a studio in Rome, where in the mid-1850s he etched a set of nine plates, some of these depicting nearby towns, the others, territorial views of the Roman Campagna. Initially printed in Italy, the set was re-published shortly after Brown's return to the United States in 1860 under the collective title *Etchings of the Campagna, Rome*. However, it was not until the rising tide of the etching revival reached American shores in the late 1870s that his etchings began to attract critical attention. Sylvester Rosa Koehler, one of the earliest and most energetic promoters of American printmaking, included Brown's *View Near Rome*, c. 1855, in his publication *American Etchings: A Collection of Twenty Original Etchings by Moran, Parrish, Ferris, Smillie, and Others* (1886). In his remarks, Koehler noted that many contemporary etchers were unaware of Brown's etchings, since the spirit that animated his art was wholly different from their own.[4] He faulted Brown's etchings for their apparent lack of freedom and individuality, qualities that were especially valued in his time; but as he wisely concluded, only certain things are possible at certain times.

Although Chapman neglected to mention etching in the first edition of *The American Drawing Book*, its rudiments were spelled out in the subsequent edition,

[2] John Gadsby Chapman, quoted in William P. Campbell, *John Gadsby Chapman, Painter and Illustrator* (Washington, D. C.: National Gallery, 1962) 62-63.

[3] Thomas Bruhn, *The American Print: Originality and Experimentation 1790-1890* (Storrs, Conn.: The William Benton Museum of Art, 1993) 64.

[4] S. R. Koehler, *American Etchings: A Collection of Twenty Original Etchings by Moran, Parrish, Ferris, Smillie, and Others* (Boston: Estes and Lauriat, 1886) not paginated.

[5] Chapman began to etch in 1848, approximately one year after the first appearance of *The American Drawing Book* (1847), which may help to explain why he neglected to mention the process in the original publication. The second edition was published after Chapman had settled in Rome and had been etching for ten years.

[6] John Gadsby Chapman, *American Drawing Book: A Manual for the Amateur and Basis of Study for the Professional Artist* (New York: J. S. Redfield, 1858) 260.

[7] Ibid.

[8] Philip G. Hamerton, *Etchings and Etchers*. (London: MacMillan & Co., 1868) vii.

[9] Ibid., xv.

published in 1858.[5] Chapman's discourse on etching, condensed to eighteen illustrated pages, was the earliest published treatise on etching written by an American author. Early in the chapter, Chapman advised those interested in taking up the needle and copper plate to "try simple subjects first," and if possible, "copy some good specimens of artist-etchings in which the management and effects of the lines are obvious, and in which there are few dark and confused masses."[6] He wisely included several examples for just this purpose. Chapman also instructed the novice to draw directly on the plate, recommending that he "not embarrass himself by attempting to reverse his copies, so that when printed they may have the same direction as the original," which became the standard procedure among etchers associated with the American Etching Revival.[7] In regards to printing, he advised would-be etchers to wipe the plate clean after the ink had been worked into the bitten lines in order to achieve an even tonality and to preserve the integrity of the drawing.

Many of the precepts Chapman outlined in his discourse on etching were rejected by etchers of the 1880s and later for being too closely allied to engraving. The etching style that Chapman and Brown employed in their works is characterized by a firmly controlled and sometimes impersonal line, the image itself evolving in totally linear terms. The even tonality found in the prints was achieved in part through the use of delicate, closely etched lines, which were combined with light stipple work. According to Robert Swain Gifford (1840-1905), who learned to etch by reading Chapman's manual, the works of Chapman and his generation were contrary to the "true spirit of etching" in which the autographic print was the ultimate achievement.

Prior to 1877 and the founding of the New York Etching Club, which is credited with ushering in the etching revival in America, the medium had suffered in the United States from its close relationship with illustration and reproductive printmaking. Only a handful of artists working in the United States had considered its potential as a possible form of artistic expression, few of them seriously. One of the sparks that ignited the etching boom in this country came from England almost ten years earlier, Philip G. Hamerton's influential bestseller *Etchings and Etchers*. The first edition sold out soon after its appearance in 1868. Artists from the Atlantic to the Pacific bought Hamerton's book, many of them endorsing his claim that etching was the free expression of pure artistic thought.[8]

Hamerton, a skilled though uninspired etcher, had received his training in the early 1860s when he was a student of the French master Auguste Delâtre (1822-1907), to whom I shall return shortly. According to Hamerton, the modern etcher was first and foremost a man, since few women possessed the proper temperament for etching. The etcher was also extremely sensitive, passionate, and direct in speech and manner. He was endowed with remarkable skills, among them the ability to extract the essential elements of nature, which he was able to transfer to the copper plate with a few spontaneous flecks of the needle. These idiosyncratic markings bore his personal feelings and sensations, which the compassionate and learned viewer could readily comprehend. As Hamerton explained, "Etching, when it is good, is always suggestive, interpretative, explanatory, but never imitative."[9] In his opinion, etching was the most honest and straightforward of all the arts, which he believed had contributed to its unpopularity with artists and the general public; as he wrote,

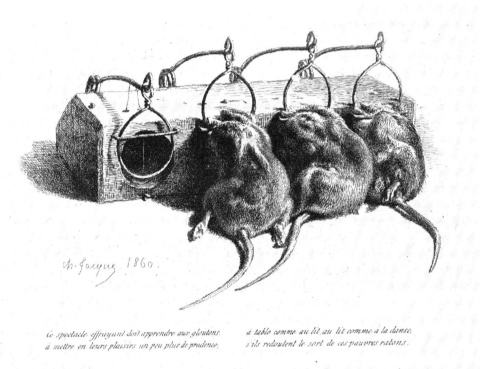

Ce spectacle effrayant doit apprendre aux gloutons,
à mettre en leurs plaisirs un peu plus de prudence,

à table comme au lit, au lit comme à la danse,
s'ils redoutent le sort de ces pauvres ratons.

Gazette des Beaux-Arts.

Imp. Delâtre

Figure 1
Charles Emile Jacque
France, 1813-1894
La Souricière, 1860
Spencer Museum of Art, The University of
Kansas: Museum purchase, Letha Churchill
Walker Memorial Art Fund, 1993.320

[10] Ibid., 59.

"People do not like plain lines that tell rude truths."[10]

Although it was written as a practical manual from which several generations of etchers obtained their knowledge of the art, the book's author had another goal, which was to make a contribution to the philosophy of etching by defining and codifying its intentions and rules. The first part of the book is devoted to etching's singular powers and qualities, the author claiming that the medium was the antithesis of such printmaking techniques as engraving, which, as he explained, was a slow and labor intensive process, with some plates requiring years and many different hands to complete. Etchings on the other hand, were to be done quickly, in one sitting if possible, before the flame of artistic creativity burned itself out. In the three following sections Hamerton examined the qualities and merits of the English, French, and Dutch schools, his selection of etchers and their works serving as proper examples of what the novice should and should not do. The final segment of the book is devoted to etching processes, with lengthy, detailed instructions on a variety of topics, from the furnishing of the etching room to the final printing of the plate; such practical information surely contributed to the immense popularity of the book. Nevertheless, the aesthetic principles that Hamerton advocated in his text were embraced by many of the artists associated with the etching revival in America. The tight and highly finished style favored by Chapman and his generation was discarded and replaced with one that allowed for the personal expression of the artist. Thus in the United States at least, the art of etching did not undergo a revival as much as a radical redefinition.

These new aesthetics, which were essentially imported from abroad, arrived in the United States in a series of cycles.[11] Hamerton's *Etchings and Etchers* appeared on the first wave and was followed by a series of groundbreaking exhibitions that introduced American etchers to the achievements of their European counterparts. The first of these occurred in conjunction with the 1876 Centennial Exhibition in Philadelphia. It was the largest exhibition of its kind to date, and attracted many aspiring etchers, who were encouraged to examine and learn from the more than two hundred etchings on display. Well over half of the prints, one hundred thirty to be exact, were by foreigners, most of them French. The remainder were American, the majority submitted by two etchers, Peter Moran (1841-1914) and Edwin Forbes (1839-1895). Among the foreign works on display were etchings by French printmakers Charles Jacque (1813-1894), Charles Meryon (1824-1868), and Maxime Lalanne (1827-1886). Lalanne wrote *A Treatise on Etching* (1866), another important and influential etching manual, which eventually made its way to the United States with Koehler's translation in 1880.

The etching revival in France was born in the early 1840s and expired in the 1880s, about the same time the etching craze erupted on this side of the Atlantic.[12] A small group of like-minded landscape painters working in the environs of Barbizon, known collectively as the Barbizon school, were arguably the first to revive interest in the needle and copper plate.[13] Charles Jacque, perhaps the most prolific printmaker of the troupe, which also included Charles-François Daubigny (1817-78), Jean-François Millet (1814-75), and Jean-Baptiste-Camille Corot (1796-1875), had worked as map engraver before trying his hand at etching. His interest in the medium was fueled by his early studies of seventeenth-century Dutch masters, etchers like Jacob

[11] Gladys Engel Lang and Kurt Lang, *Etched in Memory: The Building and Survival of Artistic Reputation* (Chapel Hill, North Carolina: The University of North Carolina Press, 1990) 53. See also: Rona Schneider, "The American Etching Revival: Its French Sources and Early Years," *The American Art Journal* (Autumn, 1982) 40-65.

[12] Lang and Lang, 33-34. The demise of the French etching revival is attributed to a variety of factors, among them the rising popularity of other print mediums, such as woodblocks, lithography, and photographic processes.

[13] For more information on this group of etchers see: Linda Hults, *The Print in the Western World* (Madison, Wisc.: University of Wisconsin Press, 1996) 529-536.

Figure 2
Charles Meryon
France, 1824-1868
L'Abside de Nôtre Dame de Paris, 1854
Spencer Museum of Art, The University of
Kansas: Museum purchase: Charles Z. Offin
Art Fund, Tom Maupin Memorial Fund, and
the Letha Churchill Walker Memorial Art
Fund, 1986.3

van Ruysdael (1628-82), Adriaen van Ostade (1610-81), and, most notably, Rembrandt van Rijn (1606-69), whose autographic technique served as an early model. Jacque devoted most of his long career to working on the copper plate and by the time of his death in 1894 he had produced almost five hundred etchings. Today he is best known for his bucolic landscapes populated with a variety of domesticated animals: cows, horses, sheep, and pigs, as well as for his descriptive portraits of rustic farmhouses, which inspired American etchers such as James Abbott McNeill Whistler.

Jacque's delightfully morbid *Souricière* from 1860 (fig. 1) can be described as a *nature morte* in the most literal sense. It was printed in the Parisian workshop of Auguste Delâtre, who transformed the art of etching with his uncommon printing techniques.[14] Delâtre pioneered the use of *retroussage* and plate tone, discovering how one could obtain a variety of effects from a single plate through selective wiping. Although Philip Hamerton considered Delâtre's printing methods a little heavy-handed at times, he conceded that there was no more intelligent printer to be found.[15] An artist in his own right, Delâtre was very sensitive to the demands of his clients, which prompted many of the printmakers who frequented his shop to insist that he pull the impressions himself. Among the many plates that passed through his presses were those created by Charles Meryon, whose haunting images of Paris stirred the imaginations of many American etchers.

Little known during his lifetime, Meryon is now regarded as one of the great masters of etching, his reputation surpassed only by the likes of Rembrandt and Whistler. A loner and paranoiac, he intentionally distanced himself from his contemporaries during his lifetime, despite the attention he received from critics Charles Baudelaire, Theophile Gautier, Victor Hugo, and others who sought to introduce his haunting images of Paris to a wider audience.[16] Meryon developed his elegant precision of line in the workshop of Eugène Bléry (1805-87), who taught his students the art of etching by having them copy paintings onto the copper plate. While under Bléry's tutelage Meryon happened upon the paintings and etchings of Reynier Nooms (1623-64), a Dutch sailor turned painter, who preferred to be known as Zeeman, the Dutch word for seaman. Although he is best known as a marine painter, specifically for harbor views of Paris, Venice, and his native Amsterdam, Zeeman was also an accomplished etcher. His highly accurate renderings of Parisian architecture, such as the series of etchings he devoted to the Louvre, exhibit a mood and freedom of style that captivated Meryon's imagination. His influence was so immediate and profound that Meryon dedicated his first set of etchings, *Eaux-fortes sur Paris* (1850-61), to his long deceased mentor.

Meryon's exquisite line work is most evident in etchings like *L'Abside de Nôtre Dame de Paris* (1854), one of his master prints (fig. 2). Rising from the banks of the Seine on the Île de la Cité, the magnificent gothic cathedral takes on a mysterious, dream-like aura. It can be understood as a symbol of medieval Paris, which would soon be radically transformed into a modern metropolis by Baron Haussmann who, working under the directives of Emperor Louis Napoleon, destroyed the "picturesque labyrinth of old Paris" in order to construct his monotonously handsome modern streets and boulevards.[17] The boatmen unloading their cargo onto the horse-drawn

[14] Lang and Lang, 31-32.

[15] Hamerton, 349-354.

[16] For critical responses to Meryon's etchings, see James D. Burke, *Charles Meryon: Prints and Drawings* (New Haven, Conn.: Yale University Art Gallery, 1974) 1-13.

[17] Frederick Keppel, "Charles Meryon: A Biographical Sketch," *American Etchers* (New York: Frederick Keppel & Co., 1886) 29.

carts in the foreground are possibly a tribute to Zeeman the painter of sailors, who included similar motifs in many of his harbor scenes. Their English counterparts can be found in a suite of etchings known as the *Thames Set* (1859), by the American expatriate James Abbott McNeill Whistler, who, along with his English brother-in-law Francis Seymour Haden (1818-1910), revitalized the art of etching in England.

It is believed that Haden was responsible for introducing Whistler to the art of etching.[18] A surgeon by profession, Haden had learned the rudiments of etching while studying medicine at the Sorbonne in the early 1840s. However, his early interest in the medium was that of an amateur, for at this time he was more concerned with collecting than creating prints. Like the etchers associated with the Barbizon school, Haden exhibited a special fondness for the works of the seventeenth-century Dutch masters, and within a few years he had amassed one of the most important collections of their works to date, including many fine impressions by Rembrandt. After witnessing Whistler's success with the *French Set* (1858, see p. 9), Haden decided to ply the needle creatively, but when he began to receive favorable notices from critics on both sides of the English Channel, the always irascible and combative Whistler became enraged and mounted an unsuccessful campaign to discredit his brother-in-law; he also ceased etching for seven years in protest.[19]

Prior to this time, etching in England had been used primarily for illustration and reproductive printmaking. As in the United States, only a few artists had considered its potential as a valid form of art. Haden, distressed by etching's subservient role in the visual arts, assumed the role of promoter and theorist, and he fought tirelessly to raise the stature of the art in England. Angered by the Royal Academy's decision to bar painter-etchers from its membership, he campaigned successfully for an alternative organization, which was realized in the establishment of the Royal Society of Painter-Etchers. Within two years of its founding in 1880, the Society had become an international body, with eight Americans elected as members in 1882. In his efforts to upgrade the respectability of its practitioners, Haden also advocated the use of the professional title "painter-etchers," a translation of the French term *peintre-graveurs*, which found general acceptance among etchers. Not surprisingly, Whistler objected vociferously to such designations, claiming that the term made as much sense as the title "barber-surgeon," which he used to describe Haden.[20] Whistler bitterly resented Haden for his self-appointed role as spokesman for the etching revival, and the professional jealousy that erupted between the two men eventually led to an irreconcilable break.

Many of the theoretical principles Haden advocated were accepted and promoted by Hamerton in his text *Etchings and Etchers*.[21] For example, Haden called attention to the inherent beauty of the etched line, claiming that the highest attainment in etching was the ability to suggest a great deal with the fewest possible strokes of the needle. He also railed against the idea of the preliminary sketch, holding that the etcher should work directly from nature and set down his personal impressions on the copper plate with the minimum amount of planning. Haden also promoted the idea (which was embraced by most modern etchers) that the finest proofs could only be pulled by the artists themselves or under their strict supervision. While Haden had assumed the role of pontiff, Whistler chose to effect a change in the art of etch-

[18] Katharine A. Lochnan, *Whistler and His Circle* (Ontario, Canada: The Art Gallery of Ontario, 1986) 12.

[19] Ibid.

[20] James Abbott McNeill Whistler, quoted in Otto Bacher, *With Whistler in Venice* (New York: The Century Co., 1909) 135.

[21] Lang and Lang, 42-43.

ing through his unprecedented experiments on the copper plate.

Following the completion of his art studies in Paris in August of 1858, Whistler traveled throughout France and Germany with his trusted colleague Ernest Delannoy, intent on completing a series of etchings he had begun earlier in the year. A set of prints resulting from the journey were published in October of that year under the title *Twelve Etchings from Nature*, more commonly known as the *French Set* (1858). The etchings attracted considerable notice, most of it positive, and the success of the portfolio launched Whistler on his career as an etcher. One of the best-known images from this series, *The Unsafe Tenement* (1858), which was printed in Delâtre's shop, shows Jacque's influence in both its subject matter and style. However, Whistler's etching style would undergo constant revision in the years that followed, his techniques changing to suit the subject or mood he sought to convey.

It is impossible to overestimate Whistler's influence on succeeding generations, for almost every American etcher who followed in his wake looked to him for instruction at some point during his/her career. More than any artist living at the time, Whistler mined the art of etching for all it had to offer. He invented new compositional formats, such as the vignette with its central focus, which was appropriated by many of his disciples. He also experimented with different biting and printing techniques, which further expanded the limits of the medium. His etchings first crossed the Atlantic in 1868, preceding Hamerton's text by a few weeks or months. They stirred considerable interest among artists and collectors when they were shown in New York and, equally important, inspired some American etchers to venture abroad.

❦

When the charter members of the New York Etchers Club first assembled on May 2, 1877, there were seventeen artists in attendance; less than half of them had any previous knowledge of etching.[22] James David Smillie (1833-1909), a skilled etcher and the club's principal organizer, had wisely arranged for a demonstration. He ground the plate and passed it to Robert Swain Gifford who drew on it and in turn passed it to Leroy Milton Yale (1841-1906) for printing. Those attending the proceedings were reportedly left spellbound, and on the second Monday of every month thereafter they came together for further instructions and support, the membership increasing slowly but steadily. Like Haden's Royal Society of Painter-Etchers, the club's ultimate goal was to raise the stature of etching in the United States. The club accomplished this in part by defining its inherent characteristics, which it borrowed from Hamerton and other sources. It also offered classes in etching and provided professional support to artists interested in the medium in the form of discussion groups, exhibition venues, and publications. In their efforts to gain respectability, the members assumed the professional title of painter-etchers, as their French and English counterparts had done earlier. Although the term gave primacy to the art of painting, it contributed greatly to legitimizing etching as a viable form of artistic expression. As Jules Dupré (1811-89), one of the forgotten pioneers of the French School, once cautioned, "artists should paint on their good days and their bad, but etch on their good ones only."[23] Within five years, similar organizations had sprung

[22] Schneider, 40.

[23] Jules Dupré, quoted in Mariana Griswold Van Rensselaer, *American Etchers* (New York: Frederick Keppel & Co., 1886) 9.

up in the United States, with etching associations located in Cleveland, Philadelphia, Boston, Brooklyn, and as far west as San Francisco.

One of the most enthusiastic and energetic supporters of the etching revival in the United States was Mariana Griswold van Rensselaer. Taking her cues from Philip Hamerton's *Etching and Etchers*, Rensselaer first outlined the mechanics of the process in her brilliantly written essay "American Etchers", which was published in the February 1883 issue of *The Century Magazine*. According to the author, etching was "infinitely freer than any other print medium" since the etching ground offered less resistance to the artist's touch than paper to the pen or pencil.[24] It not only allowed the artist to improvise upon the plate, but also captured and preserved the least idiosyncrasy of his drawing. Rensselaer's essay was illustrated with sixteen etchings created by some of the leading American etchers of the day, including one work by Mary Nimmo Moran (1842-99). Although she found the works of these etchers to be extraordinary examples of the art of etching in America, Rensselaer reserved special praise for those artists like Moran who eschewed foreign subjects in favor of recognizable American motifs. She described Whistler and his contemporaries who chose to live and work abroad as "clever workmen," whose etchings of foreign subjects "were among their least successful works."[25] Despite Rensselaer's nationalistic sentiments, a significant number of American etchers chose to go abroad during this time, and most of them returned with etchings they created during their travels, the prints finding an appreciative audience among discriminating print collectors.

As Barbara Weinberg reminds us, American art underwent a radical change in the years following the Civil War.[26] According to the author, the economic, political and philosophical upheavals that accompanied the war were largely responsible for this redefinition of American art. The moralistic and naturalistic tendencies in landscape and rural genre subjects that distinguished American art before the war were replaced by a new aesthetic that favored foreign imports. This radical redefinition of American art was prompted and financially supported by wealthy industrialists and financiers who had developed a taste for European art and culture, and painters such as William Morris Hunt (1824-79) were instrumental in bringing this new art to an American audience. With very few exceptions, American artists chose to study abroad. Their objective, according to Weinberg, was to create a national art that, though founded on European models, would answer American needs.[27]

Many of these artists sought training in Paris and Munich, which had supplanted Düsseldorf as the leading German art center in the 1860s. Frank Duveneck makes an interesting case study, for he arrived in Munich in 1870, when the Royal Academy was in a state of turmoil as the academic tradition was displaced by a new painterly style ushered in by artists like Wilhelm Leibl (1844-1900), who had recently assumed the position of leadership at the Academy. Nature was the new model, and she was to be interpreted in bold expressive brushwork that conveyed the pure enjoyment of painting. In Munich, Duveneck adopted a somber palette, derived from his studies of Franz Hals (1581/85-1666), and developed an honest, straightforward painting style that was refreshing in its frankness. Duveneck's rise within the Academy was meteoric, and by the time he left in 1873, he had received many prestigious awards.

After a short, two-year visit to the United States, Duveneck returned to the

[24] Rensselaer, 8.

[25] Ibid., 17.

[26] H. Barbara Weinberg, "Introduction," *American Etchings and American Art* (New York: Garland Publishing, 1978) 1.

[27] Ibid. See also: Michael Quick, *American Expatriate Painters of the Nineteenth Century* (Dayton, Ohio: The Dayton Art Institute, 1976) 13-45.

[28] John Ruskin, *The Stones of Venice* (London: Penguin Books, 2001)13.

gemütlichkeit of Munich with William Merritt Chase (1849-1916), who is most closely associated with the Paris school. He remained there until 1877, when he accompanied Chase and his students to Venice. Like numerous Americans before and since, Duveneck fell in love with the medieval port city immortalized in John Ruskin's *Stones of Venice* (1853). In the opening pages of his book the author described Venice aptly as a "ghost upon the sands of the sea, so weak, so quiet, so bereft of all but her loveliness, that we might well doubt, as we watched her faint reflection in the mirage of the lagoon, which was the city and which was the shadow."[28] Many of the etchers who traveled to Venice in the late nineteenth and early twentieth centuries were lured there by Ruskin's romantic sentiments.

Upon his return to Munich nine months later, Duveneck opened an art school for American and English students. However, more than sixty students of various nationalities enrolled the first year, requiring him to teach two different sessions, one for English speaking students, and another for non-English speaking students. Duveneck was a natural born teacher, and his art classes were known for the unusual and spirited camaraderie that took place between teacher and students. His most gifted pupils became known as "Duveneck's Boys."

In the winter of 1879 Duveneck went to Florence at the urging of his only female student—and future wife—Elizabeth Boott (d.1888). Many of his "boys" followed. Among the group in Florence that winter were Charles Corwin, Oliver Dennett Grover, Charles Mills, Julius Rolshoven, and Otto Bacher, who turned Duveneck's interest to etching. For two years this renegade band of painters wintered in Florence and summered in Venice. It was during their first visit to Venice, in May 1880, that they came into contact with Whistler, who was there to complete a suite of twelve etchings commissioned by the Fine Art Society of London.[29]

[29] Eric Denker, *Whistler and his Circle in Venice* (London: Merrell Publishers, 2003) 12-13.

Surprisingly, a warm and long-lasting friendship developed between the usually cantankerous Whistler and many of Duveneck's boys, who were thrilled to find themselves in his company. Otto Bacher, the most experienced etcher of the group, explained their situation in a letter to an acquaintance in the United States, writing, "We are nicely situated here—have a good view from our windows and the advantage of fellow students to look at what you are doing and helping you, besides the good influence of Duveneck and Whistler. The latter lives in our house—he seems to have taken to the boys and likes our company—it is a treat for us to see his work, I assure you. I have never been placed in a better position than now to do copper work with ten or a dozen of Whistler's coppers around my room."[30]

[30] Otto Bacher, in a letter to Harold Fletcher dated July 1, 1880, published in William W. Andrew, *Otto Bacher* (Madison, Wisc.: Education Industries, Inc., 1973) not paginated.

When Whistler had arrived in Venice on September 19, 1879—his mistress, Maud Franklin, would join him a month later—he first took a room in Palazzo Rezzonico in the Dorsoduro district near the church of Santa Maria Gloriosa dei Frari, where he remained for eight months. In June the following year, Whistler had paid a visit to the Duveneck boys, most of whom were headquartered in the Casa Jankowitz, located in the Castello district on the wide quay of the Riva degli Schiavoni. Finding these accommodations more to his liking, Whistler and his mistress moved to the Casa Jankowitz a few weeks later. Bacher, whose room was located near Whistler's, became his closest confidant. The fact that Bacher etched and that he had done so before coming to Venice, plus the fact that he owned a portable press

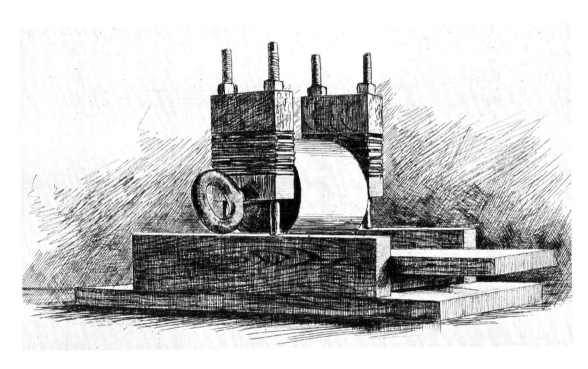

Figure 3
Drawing of a Portable Etching Press
from Hamerton's *Etchings & Etchers*, 1868

and openly admired Whistler's work, were reasons enough for the intimate friend-ship that developed between the two men; Whistler showed his appreciation by claiming Bacher as *his* pupil.

Bacher had become interested in etching in 1876, while studying art in his hometown of Cleveland. The circumstances that motivated Bacher to try his hand at etching are unknown, but it is likely that he was inspired to do so by Hamerton's *Etchings and Etchers*, a copy of which he is known to have owned. Like many of his generation, Bacher believed that sound artistic instruction could only be found abroad, and so he elected to study in Munich. He arrived there in 1878 and found the bohemian atmosphere, in which independent experimentation was combined with studies of the Old Masters, intoxicating. In the spring of 1879 he enrolled in Duveneck's painting class. He passed the summer of that year working on a suite of etchings known as the *Danube Series*, which is comprised of twenty-seven plates depicting such picturesque German villages Lustheim, Schwabelweiss, and Regensberg. Bacher wandered over the countryside that summer with a copy of *Etchings and Etchers* tucked into his knapsack for reference and a portable etching press, which he had constructed from Hamerton's specifications (fig. 3). Although the exact dimen-sions of the press are unknown, Bacher stated that it was significantly larger than the average portable press.[31]

[31] Otto Henry Bacher, *With Whistler in Venice* (New York: The Century Co., 1909) 9.

[32] Andrew, not paginated.

In the fall of 1879 Bacher accompanied Duveneck and his classmates to Florence, where he introduced many of them to the art of etching. By this time, Bacher was something of an authority on the technical processes of etching, which he imparted to his teacher and a few of his colleagues. Duveneck became enamored with the process and, despite his amateur status, produced several masterful plates during this first trip to Venice, most of which were bitten and proofed by Bacher.[32] In 1881, three of Duveneck's unsigned etchings were submitted without his knowledge to an exhibition sponsored by the Royal Society of Painter-Etchers. The etchings, which depict the Riva degli Schiavoni, received favorable comments from critics and were judged by the experts to be examples of Whistler's work in Venice. Not surprisingly, when word of this mistake reached Whistler, he became enraged.

Nowhere else had there been an atmosphere so appealing to etchers as Venice. The busy canals and quiet streets, the ornamented doorways and gardens, churches and palaces, boats and bridges, and a variety of people performing their daily tasks out of doors were all alluring subjects, and as Bacher tells it, no one had dared etch Venice before Whistler. Bacher spent most of that first summer in Venice in Whistler's company. They passed many days and hours together, each of them learning from the other. Bacher was given the privilege of watching Whistler work; he also acted as his assistant at times. He was often given the task of applying the ground to the plates, for Whistler had come to prefer Bacher's formula for wax to his own. Before coming to Venice, Bacher had employed Hamerton's positive process of biting the plates, which he demonstrated for his learned companion. However, Whistler greatly disliked the limited effects that resulted from the process and therefore continued to move the acid over the plate in the old-fashioned manner as he had always done with a gentle touch of a feather. Sometime thereafter, Bacher began to bite his plates in the same manner.

Whistler and Bacher could be seen roaming the streets and canals of Venice in search of subjects and paper for printing, both of them preferring the type of paper that could be found in old sixteenth- and seventeenth-century ledger books. When Bacher returned home one day from his wanderings with a bundle of old paper he had purchased for a mere franc, Whistler immediately arranged for a trade, swapping Bacher one of his latest proofs for a share of the paper.[33] The two men also spent many hours proofing plates on Bacher's press, and according to Bacher, most of the etchings that Whistler, Duveneck, and the "boys" produced while working in Venice were proofed on this press.[34] The warm relationship that sprang up between Bacher and Whistler was advantageous for both men. Whereas the latter gained even greater technical proficiency, the former acquired the ability to present the actual in subjective terms, which took him several more years to master.

[33] Bacher, 126-27.

[34] Ibid., 113.

Bacher remained in Venice through the fall of 1880, choosing to return to Florence for the winter. Whistler went back to London in November of the same year. However, Bacher paid several visits to Whistler in London in the years that followed, the two men remaining close friends until Whistler's death in 1903. Three years later, Bacher penned an account of their time together, which was published in the December issue of *The Century Magazine*. A second article, "Stories with Whistler," followed in May, 1907. Encouraged by the popularity of these essays, Bacher expanded on them in a book he titled *With Whistler in Venice* (1908). This engaging and highly informative narrative is packed with amusing anecdotes and detailed descriptions of Whistler's etching techniques. Profusely illustrated with reproductions of etchings they produced in Venice, the book is a remarkable resource of information for anyone interested in the history of etching.

Bacher returned the United States briefly in 1884. In the spring of that year, he submitted three etchings of Venice to an exhibition sponsored by the National Academy of Design; the asking price for the etchings ranged from $300 to $500 each. These exorbitant prices indicate that the etching craze was in full swing, which it indeed was, with artists and publishers across the country cranking out large editions of prints in order to meet the ever-increasing demands of collectors and the general public.

In France, Alfred Cadart (1828-1875), the founder of the *Société des Aquafortistes* (1862-67), was one of the earliest and most influential publishers of original etchings.[35] For approximately five years, Cadart's firm, which was located on the Rue Richelieu, published a monthly portfolio titled *Eaux-fortes modernes*, comprised of five original etchings. Each of the etchings was produced by a different artist, with etchers such as Alphonse Legros (1837-1911), Edouard Manet (1832-83), Felix Braquemond (1833-1914), Johann Barthold Jongkind (1819-91), and François Bonvin (1817-87) contributing works to the publication. In 1868, a year after the *Société des Aquafortistes* folded, these portfolios were succeeded by another monthly titled *L'Illustration nouvelle*, which Cadart's firm continued to publish until 1880. From 1874, a year before his death, to 1881, the publishing house also put out an annual album, *L'Album*

[35] J. Bailly-Herzberg, *L'Eau-forte de peintre au dix-nuevieme siècle: La Société des aquafortistes, 1862-1867* (Paris, 1972).

Cadart, which contained thirty to forty plates—some reproductive etchings, others original plates—for which the influential critic Philippe Burty wrote the prefaces. Although Cadart's heirs sought to keep the business afloat after his death, it ended in bankruptcy in 1882 as the etching revival in France came to a quiet close.

Cadart's contemporary on the other side of the Atlantic was the influential publisher Frederick Keppel (1845-1912). In the mid-1860s, Keppel, who was at that time a successful book dealer, purchased from a London dealer a set of etchings which he subsequently sold in his shop. Encouraged by the sale, Keppel turned his interest to selling prints. He opened an art gallery in New York in 1868 and by the end of the century had become one of the most important print dealers and publishers of etchings in the United States. A number of other important publishers appeared on the scene in the 1880s, among them Christian Klackner, M. Knoedler & Company, and S. R. Koehler, who, more than any other publisher at the time, sought to introduce the works of American etchers to a larger audience.

Koehler's role as theorist, publisher, and proponent of American etching cannot be overestimated. From 1879-81 he served as the editor for *The American Art Review*, a journal he founded and dedicated to popularizing the art of etching in America. Unfortunately, Koehler's publication, which was based on European journals like the *Zeitschrift für bildende Kunst* and the *Gazette des Beaux-Arts*, had a very limited audience composed primarily of print connoisseurs in the United States and abroad. During its two-year existence no issue ever sold out, and all efforts to extend its base of support ended in failure. Much to Koehler's chagrin the periodical folded. However, as Thomas Bruhn has remarked, the journal promoted not only etching but American etching, and the increase in public awareness of etching and the artists' recognition of the possibilities of etching were both legacies of *The American Art Review*.[36]

Koehler remained an indefatigable force in American etching despite the failure of *The American Art Review* and he published numerous volumes that sought to popularize the art of etching in the United States. Among his most impressive publications were *Original Etchings by American Etchers* (1883), which was the first major portfolio of etchings published in the United States, and *Etching: An Outline of Its Technical Process & Its History* (1885), a visually impressive and weighty tome that makes Hamerton's lengthy treatise look like a inexpensive pamphlet. Phyllis Peet reminds us that Koehler was also influential in promoting prints by women artists.[37] He organized the first exhibition of their works, *The Women Etchers of America*, which opened at the Boston Museum of Fine Arts on November 1, 1887. On display in the galleries were 388 etchings by twenty-three artists. The following year an enlarged version of the exhibition appeared at the Union League of New York with 509 etchings produced by thirty-five artists.

Although Koehler failed to attract enough subscribers to make *The American Art Review* profitable, interest in American etchings continued to grow, as exemplified by the large number of books that were illustrated with original etchings. One example is the exquisitely produced *Poets and Etchers*, which was published in 1882 by the Boston firm James R. Osgood & Company. As Rona Schneider has remarked, this volume "represents the finest marriage of poetry and etching in the Etching Revival period."[38] Inside the green gilded boards are sixteen poems written by such literary

[36] Bruhn, 8.

[37] Phyllis Peet, *American Women of the Etching Revival* (Atlanta: High Museum of Art, 1988) 9-10.

[38] Rona Schneider, *American Painter Etchings, 1853-1908* (New York: The Grollier Club, 1989) 12.

giants as William Cullen Bryant, Ralph Waldo Emerson, Henry Wadsworth Longfellow, and John Greenleaf Whittier, each them beautifully illustrated with an original etching by such early masters as Samuel Colman, Robert Swain Gifford, and James D. Smillie; a few of the prints depict foreign locales, such as Amalfi, Bruges, and Palestine.

As the large number of books in this genre indicates, a fashion for etchings was developing in the United States. In 1875 the sale of modern etchings made up only two percent of the total number of prints sold in the United States, but by 1883 they constituted seventy-three percent of the market.[39] The fad turned into commercial exploitation as large department stores became marketing channels for etchings and publishing houses began to operate around the clock in order to meet the high demand. This commercial exploitation encouraged mediocre talents, so that by the early 1890s anyone with acceptable drawing skills could be hired to produce etchings that inevitably found their way onto the market. In addition, inferior printing practices resulted from this unprecedented demand for etchings. For instance, when one compares two impressions of Joseph Pennell's *The Ponte Vecchio, Florence* from 1882, one printed by the artist and the other by the publishing firm Brown and Bigelow of St. Paul, Minnesota (fig. 4), the differences are striking. In the former the etched lines are clean and crisp, the areas of light and dark masterfully conceived and rendered. In the latter, which is likely the result of a photo-mechanical process and curiously bears the printed signature of the artist, many of the lines have broken down, some of them disappearing completely. The chiaroscuro so beautifully rendered in the original print has become muddied and thus ineffectual. As one might expect, with so many inferior prints flooding the market, collectors began to cut back on their purchases of etchings, choosing instead to acquire lithographs and engravings, which had not yet been tainted by commercial exploitation. In a very short time the etching fad had lost its appeal and the general public also began to withdraw its support. According to Koehler, writing in 1892, the etching revival had peaked in the mid-1880s, and was now on a downhill course.[40] However, as Lang and Lang have shown, the taste for etching never died out entirely; it only went into hibernation.[41]

By the beginning of the twentieth century there were signs of gradual recovery, much of which was due to dynamic publishers like Frederick Keppel, who sought to cultivate a more educated and discerning public. Keppel and his counterpart in Chicago, Albert Roullier, took the lead in this new enterprise. While Keppel tended to favor foreign etchings and those created by Americans working abroad, Roullier focused on "native" artists in his business. To educate the public, the two firms not only published prints, but also small informative booklets. These small pamphlets, which were written by print connoisseurs, were generally dedicated to the work of one artist and can be aptly described as sales catalogues. Illustrated with small reproductions of the artist's etchings, they also contained biographical sketches, as well as information about the etcher's personal approach to the medium. This revival of etching was also helped along by such publications as *Print Collector's Quarterly*, which was founded in 1911 by Keppel and Fitzroy Carrington, an associate. This innovative publication, which folded during the early years of World War II, sought to educate collectors and the general public by focusing on the great masters of etching and engraving, both old and modern, who were thought to be worthy of the

[39] Lang and Lang, 63.

[40] Sylvester Rosa Koehler, cited in Bruhn, 6.

[41] Lang and Lang, 62.

Figure 4
Joseph Pennell
United States, 1857-1926
Ponte Vecchio, Florence, 1882
Printed by Brown & Bigelow
Private Collection

reader's interest and financial support. The essays, written by print connoisseurs like Martin Hardie, contributed to popularizing the talents of American etchers like Ernest David Roth, Donald Shaw MacLaughlan and Herman Armour Webster.

Etching collectives, which sponsored classes in printmaking and provided new opportunities for studying prints, also sprang up across the United States. The Art Students League established one of the earliest formal classes in etching in 1906, with the assistance of Joseph Pennell, who in the following decade would take a teaching position there. Pennell's popular and influential courses in printmaking encouraged many artists of the next generation, such as Mary Huntoon, to take up etching. The Chicago Society of Etchers, which developed new ways of disseminating etchings to an ever larger public, was founded in 1911.[42] The success of the Society owed much to the efforts of its indefatigable secretary Bertha Jaques, who remained in the position for over twenty years. Most of the artists associated with this organization were drawn to etching more for a love of the art than for financial gain. Nevertheless, the Chicago Society of Etchers proved to be a profitable venture and helped to raise the stature of etchings in the United States by giving the public a place to see, study, and appreciate fine prints. They accomplished this in part by donating etchings to public institutions like the Art Institute of Chicago, and by creating an Associate Member category, where for a $5 annual subscription fee new members could gain access to most of the Society's functions. As an added incentive, each year associate members received an original print, created and signed by one of the Society's leading etchers. By the end of the decade similar organizations had sprung up throughout the country. Among the most popular and enduring were the Print Makers Society of California (1913), The Brooklyn Society of Etchers (1916) and the Print Club of Cleveland (1919). In the years following World War I there were signs of another etching revival in the United States, which was clearly indebted to the efforts of organizations like the Chicago Society of Etchers.

The second generation of American etchers to go abroad shared common interests and motives. The tradition of going to Europe for artistic training continued well into the twentieth century, with artists such as Orville Peets, John Marin, Donald Shaw MacLaughlan, and Herman A. Webster receiving instruction in the studios of Jean-Léon Gérôme, Jean-Paul Laurens and others. While studying painting, many these American students were exposed to etching either in their coursework or through their independent studies. Although some of these artists, such as Marin and Peets, would divide their time between painting and etching, others, like MacLaughlan and Webster, laid down their brushes in order to pursue careers in etching, which both men came to consider their primary form of artistic expression.

Other artists of this generation first traveled to Europe not as etchers but as soldiers. When the United States entered World War I in 1917, a large contingent of American artists enlisted in the military; among them were etchers like Samuel Chamberlain, Arthur Hall, and Kerr Eby. While most of them returned to America following the conflict, they remained only a short time. With etching tools in hand, they set out again for Europe and passed the post war years exploring some of the areas they first encountered during the war. They discovered subjects that they could not find in the United States; time-worn buildings and quaint towns and villages that

[42] Joby Patterson, *Bertha E. Jaques and the Chicago Society of Etchers* (Madison, N.J.: Fairleigh Dickinson University Press, 2002) 114-121.

had not yet embraced the modern world. Like the earlier generation of artists who went abroad, they were unencumbered by tradition and given the freedom to experiment. They felt comfortable in the bohemian circles of Paris, Munich, and London, and discovered there a sense of community and camaraderie they had not experienced in the United States. In addition, the post war economies of certain European countries, such as France and Germany, allowed Americans to live there inexpensively, since the strong American dollar went much further in these financially depressed nations.

Europe's singular treasures were featured in countless travel books and articles that multiplied exponentially during this period; they lured many artists abroad just as Twain's book had several generations earlier. Among the most popular travel accounts were those written by the Englishman E. V. Lucas, who represented the epitome of the vagabond traveler. In the early decades of the twentieth century Lucas wrote a number of influential books with variations on the title *A Wanderer in Paris* (1909), the first in the series; he also published similar accounts of his journeys to Holland, Venice, and Florence. The books, which could fit easily into one's knapsack, were highly popular with the public and were reprinted in numerous editions. Lucas' enchanting narratives likely inspired some American artists venturing abroad during the early decades of the twentieth century. Written by a knowledgeable traveler in a sometimes poetic, sometimes informal manner, they point out areas of interest, as well as offering practical advice on how to deal with the locals, such as talking the aged caretaker of an old church into letting one roam about as one wished in order to gain access to some hidden treasure.

Although Philip Hamerton held that most women did not possess either the temperament or the sensibility for etching, a significant number of enterprising American women etchers traveled abroad. As Phyllis Peet has shown, there were etching classes for women as early as 1879, when the Chicago Academy of Fine Arts was established, and institutions like the Philadelphia School of Design for Women and the California School of Design (now the San Francisco Art Institute) offered similar classes in the 1880s.[43] Despite the opportunities to learn etching at home, traveling, studying, and living abroad offered American women artists something more important. Like the painters, Cecilia Beaux (1855-1942), Elizabeth Nourse (1859-1938), and Romaine Brooks (1874-1970), they were able to assert their independence as artists and demonstrate their commitment to a career in the visual arts. While women received the same opportunities as men to see important works of art, opportunities for an equal education were few and costly. As Peets explains, women were denied access to the European free art academies during most of the nineteenth century, and thus many of them were forced to hire private instructors, which resulted in higher costs for living abroad.[44] Unless they were independently wealthy, as in Brooks' case, they encountered many obstacles.

While the history of art has drawn significant attention to the etchings of Mary Cassatt, it has, until Peets' landmark study and the efforts of independent scholars like Rona Schneider, neglected the work of many other American women etchers. Pioneers like Eliza Pratt Greatorex (1819-97), Gabriel deVaux Clements (1858-1948), Ellen Day Hale (1855-1940), and Blanche Dillaye (1851-1931), were all drawn to the

[43] Peets, 14.

[44] Ibid., 17.

landscape and architectural motifs favored by their male contemporaries, and they produced many remarkable prints in which their individual sensibilities are etched into the plate. Sadly, the etchings they created were often printed in small editions, and are known today by only a few impressions. For much of the twentieth century their contributions were deemed inferior to those of their male contemporaries, and many collectors and public institutions assigned them a marginal status. The fact that there are so few works in this exhibition by women etchers underscores the lack of attention their work received in the male dominated art world, a situation that should change as a new generation of scholars begins to explore and appreciate their individual lives and careers.

The American etchers featured in this exhibition are not unlike William Blake's wandering artist who roamed the English countryside in search of new experiences. With a little imagination and mindful observation, the sympathetic viewer can step back in time and meander down an ancient street in Rouen, contemplate the remarkable beauty of an abandoned château, or tread an empty path through a picturesque landscape lined with rustic houses and shops. By paying particular attention to the idiosyncratic marks the artists left on the copper plate, the viewer can also gain a sense of the excitement and passion that motivated them. It is the wish to record the artist's own feelings for a subject in an independent and personal manner that ultimately sets the Americans' works apart from those of their European contemporaries. As Joseph Pennell once said:

> A great etching
> by a great etcher,
> is a great work of art,
> displayed on a small piece of paper,
> expressed with the fewest vital,
> indispensable lines,
> of the most personal character;
> a true impression
> of something seen—
> something felt by the etcher,
> something he hopes some one
> may understand and care for
> as he, the artist, does.[45]

[45] Joseph Pennell, quoted in Bertha Jaques, *Concerning Etchings* (Chicago: The Chicago Society of Etchers, 1927) not paginated.

C ATALOGUE

Arch of the Conca, Perugia, 1926
Etching on laid paper
261 x 373 mm
10 1/4 x 14 5/8 inches
Spencer Museum of Art, The University of
Kansas: Anonymous Gift, 1998.193

John Taylor Arms

Born in Washington, D. C., 1887
Died in New York, New York, 1953

John Taylor Arms belongs to the second generation of American etchers to go abroad between the years 1880 and 1939 and, along with his contemporaries, he redefined yet again the art of etching in the United States. While an impressionistic sensibility remained dominant in the works of artists like Ernest Roth, Lester Hornby, and Orville Peets, Arms and fellow architect-etchers Samuel Chamberlain and Louis Rosenberg introduced a new sensibility that is almost photographic in its dispassionate realism. Arms's cool and meticulously drawn etchings, which were based on preliminary drawings from nature, set the standard for clean-lined, non-dramatic prints. Arms's drawing is so precise in prints like *Aspiration, La Madeleine, Verneuil-sur Avre* that the etchings appear to have been created with an engraver's burin. The profusion of details and the even light and dark values in this and other prints are also uncharacteristic of the aesthetics of the nineteenth-century etching revival. Yet, the autographic element so cherished by Arms's predecessors remains, for the artist's seemingly impersonal line is used to express a genuine and profound spirituality.

Arms graduated from the Massachusetts Institute of Technology School of Architecture in 1912 with an M. S. degree. He spent two years working as a draftsman for the New York architectural firm Carrer and Hastings before forming a partnership with Cameron Clark in 1914. He married Dorothy Noyes in 1913 and that same year took up etching as a hobby. Arms served in the Navy during World War I and after his discharge in 1919, he left his architectural practice in order to pursue printmaking full time. Self-taught, Arms looked to masters like Charles Meryon and James Whistler for guidance. He spent approximately the first five years of his career becoming acquainted with etching, and experimented with aquatint, drypoint, and mezzotint. *Somewhere in France* is one of Arms's early etchings; it exemplifies his interest at that time in accurately rendering the effects of light as it illuminates forms and creates shadows. As this print shows, Arms's meticulous drawing style was already firmly in place, his lifelong love for detail clearly noted in the crumbling structures lining the road. Early works like this are notable because they include human beings, which become noticeably absent in later works.

John Taylor Arms traveled abroad on many occasions, and his journeys are documented in his etchings. Around 1930 Arms and his wife Dorothy set out to explore northern Italy accompanied by their friends, the artist Arthur Heintzelman (1891-1965) and his wife Katharine. During their wanderings, Dorothy kept a journal which she used to write *Hilltowns and Cities of Northern Italy* (New York: The MacMillan Co., 1932).[1] The book, published after their return to the United States, was illustrated with fifty-six reproductions of etchings, aquatints, and drawings Arms had created during their sojourn. Among the etchings reproduced in the book was *Arch of the Conca, Perugia*. The arched passageway that frames the village, a compositional device borrowed from Whistler, was likely constructed by Roman masons after the region had been conquered and assimilated into the Empire. Arms discovered this motif while wandering along the walls of the old Etruscan city, and according to Dorothy had a difficult time finding a proper viewpoint. Etchings like this showcase Arms's technical facility. He discarded the traditional tools in favor of implements like sewing needles, which allowed him to create delicate and shallow lines. The etching's large size, the significant detail, and the painstaking line work all suggest that the great amount of time he spent creating this and all of his prints.

Arms and his small party also visited Venice, and the city with its aging medieval architecture, shimmering water, and vaporous light captured his imagination like no other did. While staying in Venice, Arms devoted at least eight major etchings to Venetian subjects, among them *The Enchanted Doorway, Venezia* (1930) and *Palazzo dell'Angelo* (1931).

In looking at Arms's *The Enchanted Doorway, Venezia*, one would never guess that the artist was surrounded by mobs of inquisitive onlookers while he was composing this work, and yet as Dorothy related, Arms also had to compete with pigeons constantly alighting on his drawing board and cooing in his ear. Characteristic of Arms's work at this time, the composition is straightforward in its frontality and rigid grid-like design. Yet, the mass and weight of the wall, which frames the "doorway to dreams," appears to dissolve in the decorative patterns of brick, stone, and sculpture.[2]

Arms also encountered obstacles when he went to produce *Palazzo dell'Angelo*. According to Dorothy, Arms searched all over Venice for a doorway worthy of a plate, and preferably one that had not been etched before. He settled on the portal to the Palazzo dell'Angelo, which was owned by an antique dealer, because it combined so many features characteristic of Venetian doorways: a fine façade, a decorative balcony, an elaborate grill in the arch, statues of fierce-looking lions on the steps, and a dirty Gothic angel high on the wall above the doorway. The biggest obstacle Arms had to overcome was working in a gondola. He discovered soon after starting work that it was illegal to tie a gondola to a post or railing, and that he could be fined ten lire if caught. Also, the site from which he had chosen to sketch was located along one of the main postal routes. Fortunately, the artist was successful in arranging for the mail boat, the Regie Poste, to blast its horn when it came within the vicinity so he could suspend drawing until the boat passed and its wake subsided.[3]

As the works in this exhibition demonstrate, Arms was a brilliant technician. He was a prolific printmaker as well and during the course of his career he produced

[1] Arms and his wife had collaborated on another book several years earlier. *Churches of France*, published by the MacMillan Company in 1929, was written by Dorothy and illustrated with fifty-one reproductions of etchings and drawings by her husband.

[2] Arms, 170.

[3] Arms, 180.

Palazzo dell'Angelo, 1931
Etching on laid paper
182 x 166 mm
7 1/8 x 6 1/2 inches
Spencer Museum of Art, The University of
Kansas: Anonymous Gift, 1998.184

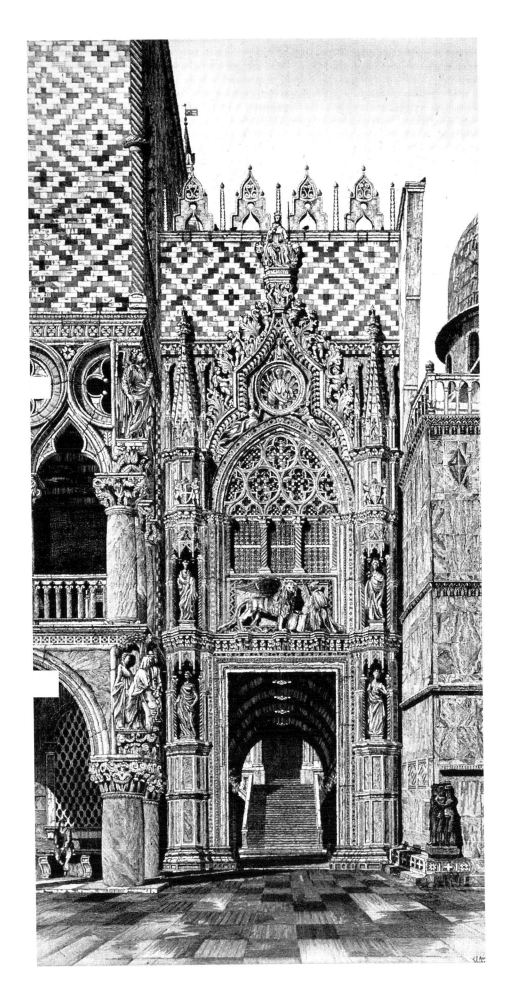

Enchanted Doorway, Venezia, 1930
Etching on laid paper
321 x 168 mm
12 5/8 x 6 5/8 inches
Spencer Museum of Art, The University
of Kansas: Anonymous Gift, 1998.177

Somewhere in France, 1919
Etching on laid paper
308 x 152 mm
12 1/8 x 6 inches
Spencer Museum of Art, The University of
Kansas: Anonymous Gift, 1998.182

more than five hundred etchings. Arms enjoyed a long and successful career in the graphic arts and, despite the fact that the demand for etchings had fallen off significantly in the early 1940s, he continued to make prints and exhibit them regularly until shortly before his death in 1953.

Sources:

William Dolan Fletcher, *John Taylor Arms, A Man for All Time: The Artist and His Work* (New Haven, Conn.: Sign of the Arrow, 1982).

Dorothy Noyes Arms, *Hill Towns and Cities of Northern Italy* (New York: The MacMillan Co., 1932).

Aspiration, La Madeleine, Verneuil-sur Avre,
1939
Etching on laid paper
397 x 254 mm, 15 5/8 x 10 inches
Spencer Museum of Art, The University of
Kansas: Anonymous Gift, 1998.194

Auf Staŭfà Brŭck, 1879
Etching on wove paper
73 x 207 mm
2 13/16 x 8 1/8 inches
Anonymous Loan

OTTO HENRY BACHER

BORN IN CLEVELAND, OHIO, 1856
DIED IN LAWRENCE PARK, BRONXVILLE, NEW YORK, 1909

One of Frank Duveneck's "boys," Otto Bacher was the most experienced etcher of the group, and when the party descended on Venice in the summer of 1880 Bacher was successful in persuading many of his colleagues to try their hand at etching (see Introduction). Shortly before his death in 1909, Bacher wrote an engaging account of that life-altering summer, titled *With Whistler in Venice* (1908).

Bacher made his first etchings in 1876 while studying art in Cleveland, and according to Sylvester Rosa Koehler, "his first experiments...resulted in the spoiling of many coppers."[4] In 1879 Bacher traveled to Munich, and in the spring, after studying briefly at the Academy, he transferred to Frank Duveneck's recently opened school. During the summer and early autumn of 1879 he wandered about Bavaria and produced a suite of twenty-seven etchings known as *The Danube Series*, the prints depicting villages and picturesque locales along the well-known river. One of the most reproduced of the series was *Auf Staüfà Brück (On Staufa Bridge),* which was published in Koehler's journal *The American Art Review*, and his book *American Etchings* (Boston: Estes and Lauriat ,1886). Bacher discovered this site near the ancient village of Donaustauf, which according to Koehler's accompanying text, "lies near the foot of the Walhalla."[5] Working with nature before him, as was his common practice, Bacher completed the plate in two sittings.

The print depicts a well-traveled wooden bridge surrounded by a few pedestrians. The dirt road in the foreground, which allows the viewer to enter the scene, rises to the bridge and the small ramshackle gatehouse. Three figures occupy the foreground, a man and child at the road's edge and a woman opposite them, burdened with the heavy load she carries upon her back. Two figures walk across the bridge, one waving a stick, as if calling to one of the figures on the road. Another figure can be detected on the far side of the bridge, which spans the narrow and quiet stream that runs across the middleground. The nearby city of Donaustauf is visible at the far right along the horizon.

Bacher was printing his own plates at this time on a press he had constructed from the specifications he found in Philip Hamerton's *Etchings and Etchers* (1868).

[4] Koehler, 11.

[5] Ibid.

Bacher was also biting his plates employing Hamerton's "positive process," in which the plate was placed in an acid bath for a set period of time. In order to produce the tonal contrasts found in *Auf Staŭfà Brŭck*, Bacher had to "bite" the plate three different times.

About a year after this etching was created Bacher traveled to Venice as one of Duveneck's boys and, shortly after arriving in the city, he became acquainted with James Abbott McNeill Whistler. A warm professional relationship quickly developed that would last a lifetime. Bacher spent many days and hours in Whistler's company, absorbing all that he could from his friend and mentor. As a result, his etching style underwent a marked change. When Koehler first saw Bacher's Venetian prints, he could not believe that were the product of the same hand that had created *The Danube Series*. In his review of the Venetian etchings, he criticized Bacher's "over-abandon," his "forced freedom," but acknowledged "one cannot help taking immense delight in these etchings."[6]

[6] Koehler cited in Andrew, not paginated.

Bacher's etching *A View from Whistler's Window* was created during the summer he spent with Whistler. It is one of forty prints that comprise *The Venetian Series*, which can be divided almost equally into marinescapes, architectural views, and genre scenes that depict washerwomen, beadstringers, and lacemakers. *A View from Whistler's Window* was, as the title implies, created in Whistler's quarters at the Casa Jankowitz, where he had secured a room with two large windows that looked out onto the lagoon toward the Doge's Palace, San Giorgio Maggiore, and the church of Santa Marià della Salute. As always, Bacher worked from the scene before him and here depicts three double-masted ships anchored in the tranquil waters of the Bacino di San Marco, their sails furled. A number of smaller boats, some with their sails unfurled, are tied to moorings alongside the Fondamenta delle Farine. Architectural landmarks like the campanile of San Marco, the Zecca, and the Doge's Palace can be detected in the background beyond the two central ships.

By this time Bacher had begun to work in states, building up a composition over a period of time by the addition of details or the reworking of certain passages, as was Whistler's practice. In *A View from Whistler's Window*, Bacher etched the background elements before strengthening the lines of the large ships and other elements with a drypoint needle. Like Whistler, Bacher had come to favor brownish inks and old papers, like those they discovered in old ledger books. This print is related to another etching from the Venetian series known as *Vessels* or *Three Ships*. The subject of *Three Ships* was also taken from Whistler's room and for a time it was known under the same title, *A View from Whistler's Window*.

Bacher's first trip to Venice came to an end in October 1880, when he followed Duveneck and his fellow classmates to Florence, where they spent the winter. He returned to Venice in the summer of 1881 and stayed for a year and a half, during which time he completed a book of twenty-one etchings of Venice, a few culled from his Venetian series, the others recent inventions. This small edition, consisting of approximately twenty books, was handmade by Bacher.

In January 1883 Bacher returned to Cleveland and shortly after accepted a teaching position at the Academy. Having been in constant contact with Whistler since leaving Venice, he traveled to London in March 1885 in order to attend

A View from Whistler's Window, 1880
Etching and drypoint on antique chain-laid
paper
118 x 319 mm
4 5/8 x 12 1/2 inches
Anonymous Loan

Whistler's second *Ten O'Clock* lecture at Cambridge. Bacher made one final trip to Venice later that year, accompanied by another painter from Cleveland, Robert Blum. His funds depleted, he returned to the United States and eventually settled in Lawrence Park, New York. Although he continued to etch, Bacher devoted an ever-increasing amount of time to painting, and was able to support his family comfortably from the sale of his paintings, prints, and occasional work as an illustrator. Bacher spent the last years of his life writing an account of his time with Whistler, excerpts of which were published in *The Century Magazine* in December 1906, and May 1907.

S O U R C E S :

William W. Andrew, *Otto H. Bacher* (Madison, Wisc.: Education Industries, Inc., 1973).

Otto Bacher 1856-1909 (Chicago: R. H. Lowe Galleries, 1991).

Otto H. Bacher, *With Whistler in Venice* (New York: The Century Co., 1909).

Sylvester Rosa Koehler, *American Etchings* (Boston: Estes and Lauriat, 1886).

En Deshabille, 1889
Drypoint on laid paper
184 x 137 mm
6 7/8 x 5 1/8 inches
Spencer Museum of Art, The University of
Kansas: Bequest of George and Annette
Cross Murphy, 1989.177

MARY CASSATT

BORN IN ALLEGHENY CITY, PENNSYLVANIA, 1844
DIED IN MESNIL-THERIBUS, OISE, FRANCE, 1926

Perhaps best known as the only American painter—and one of three women—to exhibit with the impressionists in Paris, Mary Cassatt was also an accomplished printmaker. Her introduction to graphic arts occurred in Italy, in the studios of Carlo Raimondi, with whom she studied in 1872. In the late 1870s, her close friend and colleague Edgar Degas was successful in persuading her to hone her drawing skills by working on the copper plate. Cassatt later explained the benefits of this exercise, stating that working with a needle on metal called for absolute precision in drawing from the model, and that her drawing became more disciplined since the plate would record any mistakes or corrections she had made.[7]

Cassatt began to etch seriously in 1879 and many early prints like *Waiting* (1880) combine the tonal processes of soft-ground etching and aquatint, which she gradually developed on her own. In 1880 Cassatt began to sketch friends and family members in drypoint and, working assiduously over the next several years, completed an important series of twelve drypoints—plus one extra—that were first exhibited in her 1893 exhibition at Durand-Ruel's gallery in Paris. *Baby's Back* belongs to this set of prints and, as in other works in the series, Cassatt's chosen subject is a woman and her child, and more specifically, the warm emotional bond they share. The figures are rendered entirely in lines of various widths and depths that underscore Cassatt's expertise as a draftsman. The dark drypoint line that dilineates the child's back calls to mind the surface of the human body, the touch of a baby's soft skin. As one scholar has noted, subjects like this, which employed living models, could be difficult to complete since children could not be expected to hold a pose for long.[8] Cassatt was very particular about the printing of her plates, and she would accept only clear rich impressions. She frequently called upon Auguste Delâtre to print her plates, but in 1890 she set up a printing press in her home, which she likely used to pull this impression.

Though not part of this series, *En Deshabille* is another fine example of Cassatt's work in drypoint. A young women is shown undressing. She turns her head slightly to look over her right shoulder at the intruder—the viewer—who has interrupted this private moment. As in *Baby's Back*, a great amount of open space surrounds

[7] Breeskin, 9.

[8] Breeskin, 10.

the figure, the minimal shading or modeling calling attention to the quality of Cassatt's line.

About the same time these works were produced, Cassatt began an important series of ten color aquatints that illustrate various aspects of women's lives. She was influenced by Japanese color woodblock prints, in particular the works of Kitagawa Utamaro (1753-1806) and Hosoda Yeishi (1756-1829), some of which she collected and hung in her home. As Adelyn Breeskin has observed, Cassatt "added a new chapter to the history of printmaking" with her color aquatints, which are considered among her greatest triumphs.[9] For unknown reasons, Cassatt stopped making color aquatints around 1897. However, she continued to produce drypoints until 1911 when she abandoned printmaking altogether.

[9] Ibid.

S O U R C E S:

Adelyn Breeskin, *The Graphic Art of Mary Cassatt* (New York: The Museum of Graphic Arts and Smithsonian Institution Press, 1967).

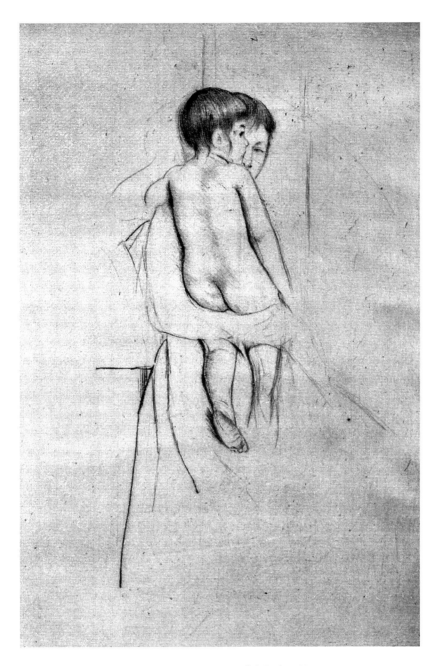

Baby's Back, 1890
Drypoint on laid paper
234 x 164 mm
9 3/16 x 6 7/16 inches
Spencer Museum of Art, The University of
Kansas: Bequest of George and Annette
Cross Murphy, 1989.178

A Country Road, 1933
Drypoint on Japan paper
198 x 259 mm
8 x 10 3/8 inches
Spencer Museum of Art, The University of
Kansas: Anonymous Gift, 1998.260

SAMUEL CHAMBERLAIN

BORN IN CRESCO, IOWA, 1895
DIED IN MARBLEHEAD, MASSACHUSETTS, 1975

[10] Samuel Chamberlain, "Etching as a Medium of Architectural Expression," 21.

Samuel Chamberlain once wrote, "There is something about the atmospheric vibrancy of an etching which imparts a peculiar and irresistible life to architectural drawing, something in an acid-bitten copper furrow which often has a greater expressiveness than mere pen or pencil lines."[10] Yet Chamberlain etched very few copper plates, for he favored the immediacy and freedom of drawing that is more characteristic of the lithographic pencil and the drypoint needle. Whether his subject was taken directly from nature or transferred to the plate from a preliminary drawing, Chamberlain sought to preserve the integrity of the original sketch in his remarkable drypoints.

An architect by training, Chamberlain had a passion for drawing that eventually led him in the direction of the graphic arts. His education at the Massachusetts Institute of Technology School of Architecture, 1915-16 and 1919-20, was interrupted by military service during World War I. Stationed in France, Chamberlain lost his heart to the country and its people; he traveled there frequently throughout his life, and on several occasions remained for prolonged periods of time. In 1924 Chamberlain published his first portfolio of prints, *Vingt Lithographies du Vieux Paris (Twenty Lithographs of Old Paris)*, and approximately a year later he etched his first copper plate; Chamberlain was essentially self-taught in both mediums. In his early etchings one can discern the artist's determination to master the mechanics of the medium, and Chamberlain's task was complicated by his decision to maintain the correct orientation of the subject before him, which required that he learn to draw backwards. He eventually acquired the mental dexterity to work from nature and maintain the correct orientation, as seen in *A Country Road*, but Chamberlain preferred to work from preliminary drawings for architectural subjects like *Cathedral of Sens*, which allowed for greater accuracy and produced a more controlled effect, the virtues of which he questioned. Yet, as these prints from the early 1930s demonstrate, Chamberlain had abandoned etching in favor of drypoint. According to Chamberlain the drypoint process held numerous advantages; among other things it allowed for a greater freedom of drawing, it required no acid bath, and it was the only sketching medium "unimpeded and unhurt by rainfall."[11] Although Chamberlain

[11] Chamberlain, "How to Make a Drypoint," 23.

The Abandoned Château, 1934
Drypoint on gray laid paper
201 x 242 mm
7 15/16 x 9 3/4 inches
Spencer Museum of Art, The University of
Kansas: Anonymous Gift, 1998.261

would turn to lithography off and on throughout his career in the graphics arts, he most prized the effects wrought by the drypoint needle, believing that it held a peculiar charm for the architect.

[12] Narcissa Gellatly Chamberlain, 15.

Chamberlain was also known for his unique perceptions of beauty which, according to his wife Narcissa, "he never failed to find in almost any circumstance."[12] Chamberlain's subject for *A Country Road* was a narrow roadway near St. Firmin in the Île-de-France. It is late afternoon on a summer day, and the large trees cast long shadows over the dusty roadbed. The muffled sounds of the horse-drawn cart travel quietly over the dirt road, which leads to a large magnificent château in the distance. The velvety lines produced by the drypoint needle are particularly well-suited to rendering the foliage blasted by the bright summer sunlight. With the drypoint needle Chamberlain was also able to produce a wide range of tones that contribute to the convincing interplay of light and dark, all while drawing backwards.

Chamberlain's virtuosity with the drypoint is also apparent in prints like *Cathedral of Sens* and the remarkable *The Abandoned Château*, even though they were based on preliminary drawings. The subject of the latter print was discovered near Fougères, Touraine in eastern Brittany, and although the structure was unidentified by the artist, the print possibly depicts a section of one of the best known landmarks in the region, the Château de Fougères, which is comprised of thirteen rounded towers topped by pinnacles and constructed of walls ten feet thick. The structure Chamberlain depicted has been left to the elements, yet remains in a remarkable state of preservation. The lawn is overgrown and unmanicured, leafless vines creep up the rough stones of the tower, and the clock, protected by the weathered eaves of the roof, has stopped at 11:40. Chamberlain's lines vary in width, depth, and length, and each fulfills a specific purpose. In drypoints like *The Abandoned Château* Chamberlain clearly demonstrated his mastery of the medium with his ability to convey depth, textures, and the interplay of light and dark.

When the market for prints ceased in the 1940s, Chamberlain's interest turned to photography, with which he had experimented earlier, and he sought to master that medium with the same zeal that had characterized his printmaking career. Chamberlain continued to travel. He undertook several epicurean tours of France, Great Britain, and Italy, and collected information for a series of books. The first, *Bouquet de France*, was published in 1949, followed by *Italian Bouquet* (1958), and *British Bouquet* (1962). Chamberlain's engaging autobiography, *Etched in Sunlight*, illustrated with his prints and photographs, appeared in 1968. He remained active and passed the last decade of his life gathering material for two more books, *New England Rooms 1639-1863* (1972), which he wrote in collaboration with his wife, and *Old Marblehead*, which was published after his death in 1974.

S O U R C E S :

Samuel Chamberlain, "Etching as a Medium of Architectural Expression," *The Prints of Samuel Chamberlain N. A.* (Boston: Boston Public Library, 1984) 21-23.

Samuel Chamberlain, "How to Make a Drypoint," *The Prints of Samuel Chamberlain N. A.* (Boston: Boston Public Library, 1984) 25-27.

Narcissa Gellatly Chamberlain, *The Prints of Samuel Chamberlain N. A.* (Boston: Boston Public Library, 1984) 15.

Cathedral of Sens, 1930
Drypoint on laid paper
273 x 181 mm
10 3/4 x 7 1/8 inches
Spencer Museum of Art, The University of
Kansas: Museum purchase, 1972.269

Venice, 1880
Etching & drypoint on wove paper
200 x 124 mm
7 7/8 x 4 7/8 inches
Spencer Museum of Art, The University of
Kansas, 00.482

CHARLES ABEL CORWIN

BORN IN NEWBURGH, NEW YORK, 1857
DIED IN CHICAGO, ILLINOIS, 1938

Having committed himself to a career in the visual arts, Charles Corwin enrolled at the Cooper Union School of Art in New York City in 1875. Seeking further instruction he traveled to Germany, and from 1877 to 1879 Corwin studied at the Munich Royal Academy. Soon afterwards, he joined Frank Duveneck's school, which had opened in 1878. As one of "Duveneck's boys" from 1879-1881, Corwin resided in Italy, passing the cold damp winters in Florence and the warm summer months exploring the wonders of Venice.

Like many in the group, Corwin experimented with the art of etching. However, his interest in the medium appears to have waned soon after he left Duveneck's circle. The number of plates Corwin produced during his Italian sojourn is unknown, though it is believed that they are few. His best-known work from his stay in Venice is a monotype of Whistler (Metropolitan Museum of Art, New York), which shows the celebrated artist in a private moment, his posture and demeanor suggesting that he is at work on an etching or pastel. Monotypes such as this were a favorite pastime for members of the group, many of whom employed the medium primarily for portraiture. These one-of-a-kind prints were known as "Bachertypes" among the members of Duveneck's circle for the simple reason that they were printed on Otto Bacher's press.

Whereas many of his colleagues focused their attention on recording the architectural wonders of the ancient city, Corwin appears to have been more attracted to genre subjects, as can be seen in his etching titled *Venice* (1880). The print depicts six boys watching a man swimming in a narrow canal lined with gondolas. The swimmer bears a strong resemblance to Whistler, who was known for taking daily baths in the lagoon. The buildings that line the canal are linked by the footbridge in the background; the mast of a great sailing ship rises above the rooftops. It is likely that Bacher printed this etching on his press; the heavily inked plate and use of *retroussage* were characteristic features of his Venetian prints.

Corwin left the group in 1881 and, following in the footsteps of such celebrated American painters as Charles Willson Peale (1741-1827) and John Vanderlyn (1775-

1852), he decided to specialize in creating illusionistic backgrounds for wildlife dioramas after his return to the United States. He was hired as a habitat constructor for Chicago's Field Museum of Natural History in 1903, and in the years that followed, Corwin produced similar works for the Iowa State University Museum and the Los Angeles County Museum of Natural History. In later years Corwin divided his time equally between his responsibilities as a staff artist for the Field Museum and as an instructor at the Art Institute in Chicago, his work in wildlife habitat reconstruction inspiring a second generation of diorama painters.

S O U R C E S :

Eric Denker, *Whistler and His Circle in Venice* (London: Merrell Publishers Limited, 2003).

Karen Wonders, "The Illusionary Art of Background Painting in Habitat Dioramas," *Curator* Vol. 33 no. 2 (June, 1990) 90-118.

The Rialto, 1883
Etching on Whatman paper
286 x 475 mm
11 1/4 x 18 7/8 inches
Spencer Museum of Art, The University of
Kansas: Museum purchase, The Peter T.
Bohan Art Acquisition Fund, 2003.108

FRANK DUVENECK

BORN IN COVINGTON, KENTUCKY, 1848
DIED IN CINCINNATI, OHIO, 1919

Frank Duveneck devoted twenty-three of his thirty known etchings to images of Venice, and his interpretations of the fabled city are unlike any others. In Duveneck's etchings, created between 1880-85, the burning light of a summer's day washes over the medieval architecture, with the city's famed canals, rivas, and bridges providing a spectacular backdrop for the flurry of human activities that he masterfully captured in his prints. Etchings like *The Rialto* are elaborate and crowded compositions, which can reward the patient viewer with a seemingly endless supply of fresh and intoxicating details that enlarge this vicarious experience of Venice.

In 1880 enrollment at Duveneck's art school in Munich had dwindled to fewer than forty students, and he saw this as a prime opportunity to take a small group of them to Venice for the summer; these students became known as "Duveneck's Boys." A member of the party, Otto Bacher, had recently taken up etching and was successful in encouraging others in the group to try their hand at the medium. Like most of them, Duveneck took his early lessons from Bacher, who also served as his chief assistant; Bacher applied the ground to Duveneck's plates, oversaw the biting of the plates, and proofed most of them as well. No member of the group exhibited the remarkable facility for etching that Duveneck did, and despite the critical success his prints received, he considered fewer than a dozen of them to be important.

Duveneck's etching style underwent a noticeable change in the summer of 1883. Prior to that time he had worked primarily on copper plates, the etchings varying in size. Early works like *Fishing Quarter, Venice* and *The Archway*, both from 1880, are distinguished from his later etchings by their vignette-like motifs and delicate drawing. In 1883 Duveneck began to work on zinc plates, and his compositions became noticeably larger and congested with numerous figures going about their daily life, as in *The Rialto*. His drawing and etching became increasingly vigorous, the lines appearing both spontaneous and highly controlled, as if fulfilling a specific function. Passages are shaded heavily in a painterly manner that resembles his impressionist painting technique.

The Rialto is a fine example of Duveneck's late style. One of the most recognized bridges in the world, the Rialto takes its name from *rivo alto* (high bank). It was one of the first areas of the city to be inhabited, and was initially a banking district before becoming the bustling market neighborhood it is today. The arcaded stone bridge, which has become a symbol of Venice, replaced an earlier wooden structure and was completed in 1591. Until the wooden bridge was built near the Accademia in 1854, the Rialto was the only means by which inhabitants could cross the Grand Canal on foot. Few visitors leave Venice without having crossed the Rialto, which provides an ever-changing view of life on the busy waterway.

Duveneck returned to the United States in 1888 after the death of his wife Elizabeth Boott; the couple had been married only two years. He settled once again in his adopted hometown of Cincinnati and accepted a teaching position at the Art Academy. In 1915 Duveneck donated all of his uncancelled plates and many of the impressions in his possession to the Cincinnati Art Museum, where his co-worker Louis Henry Meakin and pupil Herman H. Wessel later pulled some additional impressions of the uncancelled plates. These prints were stamped on the reverse "Cincinnati Museum Association/Printed by H. H. Wessel and L. H. Meakin" and a number of these were signed by the artist, Frank Duveneck. *The Rialto* in the Spencer's collection was printed earlier, most likely while the artist was working in Venice, for it is printed on Whatman paper and bears the signature F. Duveneck, identifying features of the etchings he produced abroad.

S o u r c e s:
Emily Poole, "The Etchings of Frank Duveneck," *The Print Collector's Quarterly* Vol. XXV no. 3 (October, 1938) 313-31.

Emily Poole, "Catalogue of the Etchings of Frank Duveneck," *The Print Collector's Quarterly* Vol. XXV no. 4 (December, 1938) 446-63.

Edge of the Sahara, 1922
Etching on wove paper
117 x 315 mm
4 9/16 x 12 3/8 inches
Spencer Museum of Art, The University of
Kansas: Anonymous Gift, 1998.325

KERR EBY

BORN IN TOKYO, JAPAN, 1889
DIED IN NORWALK, CONNECTICUT, 1946

Kerr Eby first visited Europe as an American soldier. Motivated by youthful idealism and patriotism, he was among the first to enlist when the United States entered World War I in 1917. Disillusionment soon followed; the horrific experiences of modern warfare inflicted a deep wound on his psyche that never fully healed. Stationed in the north of France, Eby served as a driver for the Ambulance Corps before he was assigned to the 40th Engineers, Artillery Brigade, Camouflage Division, which was responsible for protecting artillery at the front. He thus witnessed the hostilities first-hand, and recorded his keen observations of the conflict in numerous sketches, many of which he later turned into prints. Eby returned to this subject for many years afterwards, as if to exorcise from his memory the haunting impressions of the war.

Eby participated in several notable military campaigns, among them the Saint-Mihiel Drive, an important American counter-offensive against the German forces, which took place in northern France. *September 13, 1918, St. Mihiel (The Great Black Cloud)*, Eby's finest etching, is a unsettling visual narrative of this crusade. Created in 1934, approximately sixteen years after the event, this bleak commentary on the tragedy and senselessness of war is rooted in the artist's personal experiences. Like many of Eby's other illustrations of the Great War, it is a nightmarish representation of organized warfare, a testimony to "things seen and felt and never lost."[13] In 1936 Yale University Press published the artist's most complete anti-war statement, *War*. In the passionate foreword, which introduces the twenty-eight images of war that follow, Eby urged the world to stop World War II, which he saw looming on the horizon.

It is believed that Eby, whose parents were Canadian missionaries, was a self-taught etcher. He may have received his first introduction to the medium from his uncle Frederick Keppel, whose New York City gallery would later publish most of his graphic work. In 1907, Eby moved to New York to pursue a career in the visual arts. He attended the Pratt Institute in Brooklyn before moving on to the Art Students League in 1910, where he studied under George Bellows and George Bridgeman. Eby honed his graphic skills by working as an illustrator, and contributed regularly

[13] Keppel, 85.

Foggy Morning, Brittany, 1930
Etching on wove paper
176 x 257 mm
6 15/16 x10 1/16 inches
Spencer Museum of Art, The University of
Kansas: Anonymous Gift, 1998.324

to such publications as *Harper's Monthly*, *Scribner's*, and *Time*. From 1913 to 1917 he passed the summer months at an art colony located in Cos Cob, Connecticut, and there met the American impressionist painter Childe Hassam. Although Hassam was thirty years his senior, the two men developed a close friendship, with Eby acting as Hassam's etching instructor.

Eby enlisted in the war effort June 19, 1917, and returned to the United States in February, 1919 a disillusioned young man. Somewhat surprisingly, given the horrors he witnessed as a soldier, he set out again for Europe a year later, and traveled throughout France and North Africa, returning to the United States in 1921. He kept a sketchbook throughout this first post-war journey, which ultimately inspired prints like *Edge of the Sahara* (1922). Eby generally worked out the compositions for his prints in drawings, which he later transferred to the plate. This work is notable in that it represents the artist's first experiments with plate tone, as seen in the light film of ink deposited along the top and bottom edges.

Oaks in Windsor Park (1927) and *Foggy Morning, Brittany* (1930) derive from Eby's third trip abroad; from 1924 to 1925 he wandered over Great Britain and northern France collecting subjects for his graphic work. The former depicts a section of a three-mile grove of trees that connects Great Windsor Park to Windsor Castle. As in most of the artist's best prints, the goal here was to convey a personal experience rather than a mere depiction of a place or event. In works like *Oaks in Windsor Park*, nature assumes spiritual and symbolic qualities, the aged trees expressing a vital life force in their twisted trunks and searching limbs. *Foggy Morning, Brittany* (1930) pictures a small group of locals who have congregated at a stone sea wall, all of them gazing out at the fishing boats either moored or moving about the tranquil harbor. They appear to be waiting for the fog to lift so that they might go about their daily business, as suggested by the man at the far left who balances an oar on his right shoulder. This etching is related to another from the same year, *Early Morning, Brittany*, which represents a family of fisherman departing for a day's work on the sea, all of them burdened by the large wooden oars they too balance on their shoulders.

The late 1930s was perhaps the most fruitful period of Eby's career, for he produced many of his most accomplished etchings during this time, some revisiting his World War I experiences, a great many more depicting the peaceful snow-blanketed hills in and around his home in Westport, Connecticut.

Despite his strong anti-war stance, Eby sought unsuccessfully to enlist in the military service when World War II erupted. However, he landed a position as an artist correspondent for Abbott Laboratories and was commissioned to produce illustrations showing the use of medicine in the battlefield. Eby traveled throughout the Pacific with a company of Marines. He participated in the invasion of Tarawa and the jungle fighting in Bougainville and recorded these wartime experiences in numerous photographs and sketches. Some of these works formed the nucleus of *Marines In Action*, a group of thirty charcoal and wash drawings that were first exhibited in May 1945 at the Associated American Artists Gallery in New York City. In keeping with his anti-war position, the drawings are gruesome representations of armed conflict, the reality of modern warfare. It has been suggested that this latest wartime episode hastened Eby's death in 1946, for he was noticeably weakened by the experience.[14]

[14] Giardina, 11.

One of only a handful of artists to produce works that depicted important events from both World Wars, Eby also created many timeless images of nature's magnificence. As one writer has aptly described Eby's graphic work, "In his art he bared his soul, sharing things of great beauty and intense pain. His prints convey his heartfelt beliefs and emotions, and portray all that was important to him."[15]

[15] Ibid.

S O U R C E S :

Bernadette Passi Giardina, *Kerr Eby: The Complete Prints* (Bronxville, N.Y.: M Hausberg, 1997).

Dorothy Keppel, "Kerr Eby," *The Print Collector's Quarterly*, Kansas City, Mo., (February, 1939) 83-95.

Kerr Eby, *War* (New Haven, Conn.: Yale University Press, 1936).

Oaks in Windsor Park, 1927
Etching on wove paper
201 x 347 mm
7 7/8 x 13 5/8 inches
Spencer Museum of Art, The University of
Kansas: Anonymous Gift, 1998.326

Cathédrale Naturelle (Suffolk, England), 1929
Drypoint on laid paper
137 x 252 mm
5 7/16 x 9 15/16 inches
Spencer Museum of Art, The University of
Kansas: Anonymous Gift, 1998.354

Gerald K. Geerlings

BORN IN MILWAUKEE, WISCONSIN, 1897
DIED IN NEW CANAAN, CONNECTICUT, 1998

In 1922 Gerald Geerlings was working as an architect for the firm of York and Sawyer in New York City. The recently hired Louis Rosenberg had just returned from Europe with a portfolio of etchings he had produced while studying abroad. Inspired by his Rosenberg's accomplishments, Geerlings decided to try his hand at etching and, aside from a few rudimentary classes at the Royal Academy in London, taught himself to etch by reading Ernest Lumsden's popular manual *The Art of Etching*, first published in 1924. A meticulous etcher, Geerlings' favorite motif was the American city in transition, in particular the cities of Chicago and New York, where the skylines were forever being altered by the new commercial architecture of the skyscraper. Geerlings once described his etchings as distilled portraits of the American cityscape, and as one critic has written, they are in essence a romantically inspired "combination of the imagined and the observed."[16]

[16] Czestochowski, 10.

Between 1928 and 1932 Geerlings crossed the Atlantic on many occasions, dividing his time between London and New York. It was during this period that he mastered the art of etching. In London Geerlings worked primarily on American motifs and created some of his most exquisite etchings, prints like *Black Magic* (1929), *Jeweled City* (1931), and *The Vertical Mile* (1932), which showcase his accomplishments with aquatint. The etching *Cathédrale Naturelle (Suffolk, England)* is one of three plates devoted to a foreign subject, and though different in technique and mood from Geerlings' American cityscapes, the print attests to his mastery of the medium.

Cathédrale Naturelle (Suffolk, England) is one of Geerlings' rare landscapes. Utilizing the soft lines produced by the drypoint needle, Geerlings created a print that is exceptionally rich in its chromatic range, and suggests a familiarity with Rembrandt's landscapes. The shimmering light of daybreak that washes over the silent countryside softens some forms, such as the Gothic cathedral in the distance, which becomes almost translucent. Other elements become more pronounced, such as the shade trees occupying the foreground, which cast long dark shadows. Geerlings' resplendent light invests the entire landscape with a palpable atmosphere, which suggests a cool summer morning heavy with dew. In this print nature's diverse elements are endowed with spiritual associations. Like all of Geerlings etchings, the composition was worked out in many preliminary drawings. He devoted a great amount of time to each of his etchings and generally produced small editions of his works; *Cathédrale Naturelle (Suffolk, England)* is one of thirty-seven impressions printed with the assistance of Charles Welch.

When the market for prints collapsed in the early years of the Great Depression, Geerlings abandoned etching and resumed his career as an architect. He specialized in domestic architecture and regularly contributed articles to such publications as *House and Garden, House Beautiful* and *Better Homes and Gardens,* his essays offering homeowners advice on how to improve the appearance of their homes and reduce costs. Geerlings returned to printmaking in 1975 after a forty-three year absence, and this time became interested in lithography. The rich diversity of tonal gradations and surface textures characteristic of Geerlings' etchings were carried over into his work in lithography, though at times less successfully. As with his etchings, Geerlings' preferred subject matter was the American city bathed in expressive light and atmosphere.

S O U R C E S :

Joseph S. Czestochowski, *Gerald K. Geerlings*, (Cedar Rapids, Iowa: Cedar Rapids Art Association, 1984).

Scheveningen, c. 1880s
Etching on satin
100 x 160 mm
4 x 6 inches
Spencer Museum of Art,
The University of Kansas, 00.494

Robert Swain Gifford

Born in Nonamesset, Massachusetts, 1840
Died In New York, New York, 1905

Robert Swain Gifford took up the etcher's needle in his early teens while living in New Bedford, Massachusetts. Self taught, he took his lessons from Charles Gregory's *Dictionary of the Arts and Sciences* (1815-16) and later, John Gadsby Chapman's popular *American Drawing Book* (1858), in which only the rudiments of etching are outlined. In 1865, the twenty-five year-old Gifford settled in New York City and soon after arriving he published his first plates, *The Naushon Island Set*; four of the etchings depict ancient trees in and around New Bedford. The set found an appreciative audience; fifteen years later Gifford was considered one of the preeminent etchers in the United States, his reputation secure until his sudden death in 1905.

Gifford began drawing at an early age. A sympathetic neighbor, Mrs. Swain, took an active interest in the boy, and provided him with the encouragement and financial means to support his art. While living in New Bedford, he studied under the romantic marine painter Albert van Beest (1820-60), who had moved to neighboring Fairhaven in 1854. Believing that his skills were sufficiently developed, Gifford moved to Boston in 1864 to ply his trade. He soon realized that New York City offered more advantages to struggling artists and so he decided to relocate there the following year. Gifford shared a studio with Samuel Coleman (1832-1920), himself an accomplished etcher, in the Dodworth Building on 5th Avenue and 26th Street. In March 1866, he sent three paintings to the National Academy of Design for their annual exhibition; the academy showed their approval by electing him an Associate later that year.

Gifford's life-long love for travel was born in the summer of 1869, when he headed to the western United States to gather material for one his most important commissions, the illustrations for three articles in *Picturesque America*, a forty-eight part serial published by D. Appleton & Co. beginning in 1872. The Suez Canal opened to great fanfare in the fall of 1869, inciting Gifford and friend Louis Comfort Tiffany to embark on a tour of Europe and North Africa. After arriving in England, they made their way through France, Spain, Italy, and Egypt, but the bulk of Gifford's work from the this trip was devoted to Egyptian subjects. In 1873, two years after his return to the United States, Gifford married Francis Elliot; accompanied by his new wife, he set out for another tour of Europe. The couple remained abroad two years, Gifford spending a great deal of the time collecting material for his art.

Soon after their return to the United States in 1875, Gifford's early interest in etching was reawakened. At the same time he pursued his painting. Fascinated as he was by science, technology, chemistry, engineering, astronomy, and photography, subjects on which he read widely, Gifford's interest in etching seems quite natural. He became one of the founding members of the New York Society of Etchers and was elected to the Royal Academy of Painter-Etchers. His etchings range in subject matter from the coal pockets of New Bedford to the barren deserts of Tangiers. The plates based on his European adventures were taken from sketches made abroad. Although he continued to indulge his love for far off places, in the 1880s Gifford settled into his newly constructed home in Nonquitt, Massachusetts, site of a recently formed summer art colony near his boyhood home of New Bedford. Thereafter, he spent summers in Nonquitt and winters in New York City.

Gifford's etching *Palestine* served as an illustration for James Greenleaf Whittier's poem of the same name, both published in *Poets & Etchers* (1882); he created three other etchings to accompany J. R. Lowell's *Summer Storm* and Henry Wadsworth Longfellow's *The Baron of St. Castine* and *Flowers*. *Palestine* is a fine example of Gifford's working technique. All of the lines are of equal depth, which is achieved by bathing the plate once in the acid. Only the lines that hold ink are printed, for Gifford eschewed such special effects as plate tone and *retroussage*. The freedom of the drawing in this work is consistent with the loose style advocated by the founders of the etching revival. Only the most salient details are noted, yet they are enough to evoke the exotic locale.

Gifford employed a slightly tighter drawing style in *Scheveningen*, which is print-ed on satin, a common practice at the time, since many artists and their publishers liked the shimmering effects produced by the material, which seems particularly suit-ed to marine subjects like this. The quaint fishing village of Scheveningen, one of the most popular resorts along the Netherlands coast, has long attracted vacationers. The original town was drowned by the sea in 1570 and eventually rebuilt further inland. Its development resulted from the building of a road from The Hague in 1665, though it was not until 1715 that the first resort was built. A formal bathing ground appeared in 1818, and between 1896 and 1900 a sea wall was constructed. Although the village suffered significant destruction during World War II, a strong fishing industry still thrives there today.

The number of etchings Gifford produced during his career is unknown, though most estimates suggest no more than 75 plates. While many of his works were print-ed commercially for *The American Art Review*, a small edition of fifteen etchings printed on Japanese paper and signed by the artist were available to discerning collectors. It is not known whether Gifford printed the plates bearing his signature or whether another printer was responsible.

S O U R C E S :
Elton W. Hall, *R. Swain Gifford 1840-1905* (New Bedford, Mass.: Old Dartmouth Historical Society, 1974).

Palestine, 1882
Etching & chine collé
184 x 129 mm
7 3/8 x 5 1/8 inches
Spencer Museum of Art, The University
of Kansas: Gift of Jim and Virginia Moffett,
2003.80

Nôtre Dame, Paris, not dated
Etching on wove paper
228 x 183 mm
9 1/6 x 7 1/4 inches
Collection of Jim and Virginia Moffett

Gustav Frederick Goetsch

Born in Gaylord, Minnesota, 1877
Died in St. Louis, Missouri, 1969

Despite a long and varied career in the visual arts as a painter, printmaker, and teacher, Gustav Goetsch is little known today; information regarding either his travels or his etchings is sketchy at best. Goetsch began his art studies at the Minneapolis School of Fine Art under the tutelage of the American socialist painter Robert Koehler (1850-1917), who was also an accomplished etcher. It is likely that Goetsch learned to etch while studying with Koehler. Goetsch eventually made his way to the New York School of Art and the painting classes of William Merritt Chase and Charles Beckwith. Like many of his contemporaries, Goetsch soon felt the tug of Europe, and in the mid-1890s he set out for Paris. He attended the Académie Julian and later studied with the French symbolist painter Jacques-Emile Blanche (1861-1942). Goetsch returned to the United States prior to the outbreak of World War I, and exhibition records indicate that he exhibited his works frequently, his brightly colored paintings and woodblock prints garnering many awards. Although he was comfortable in the art circles of Paris and New York, Goetsch returned to the Midwest in the late 1910s. He settled there permanently, and held teaching positions at the Minneapolis School of Fine Art and Washington University in St. Louis.

Almost every American etcher who traveled to Paris from 1880 to 1939 devoted at least one copper plate to Nôtre Dame. Rising majestically from the Île de la Cité on a site that once belonged to an ancient Roman temple, the magnificent twelfth-century gothic cathedral still dominates the Paris skyline. Pope Alexander III laid the first stone in 1163, and it took approximately 170 years to complete the structure. Ransacked by French revolutionaries who had banished organized religion, the medieval cathedral became a temple to the Cult of Reason in the early 1790s; from 1795-1802 it was used to store wine. Napoleon Bonaparte restored religious practice in 1804, the same year he crowned himself emperor in Nôtre Dame. The famed French architect Eugène Viollet-le-Duc was responsible for its restoration.

Goetsch's *Nôtre Dame, Paris*, invites a comparison with Charles Meryon's masterful etching of the same subject (fig.3), with which he was certainly familiar. For his rendering of the cathedral, Goetsch took up a position on the right bank of the

Seine, approximately half way between the Pont St. Louis and the Pont de la Tournelle. Meryon's viewpoint was taken from the left bank, just beyond and to the east of the Pont de Archevêché. Though both artists depicted laborers at work on the banks of the Seine, it is the majestic cathedral that commands the viewer's attention. Rather than represent the west façade with its imposing towers, both artists focused their attentions on the cathedral's impressive *chevet*; the flying buttresses, designed by Jean Ravy, spanning fifty feet at the east end. The 293-foot spire over the crossing, a feature of Viollet-le-Duc's restoration, is missing from Meryon's etching, which predates Goetsch's print by some forty years. The masterful interplay of light and shadow in Meryon's etching lends a sense of mystery to the great cathedral, which takes on a more benign presence in Goetsch's print.

S O U R C E S:

Michael Conforti, ed., *Minnesota 1900: Art and Life on the Upper Mississippi 1890-1915* (Newark, N.J.: University of Delaware Press, 1994).

The Lido, Venice, 1888
Etching on Japan vellum
227 x 410 mm
8 15/16 x 14 3/8 inches
Collection of the Illinois Historical Art
Project

OLIVER DENNETT GROVER

BORN IN EARLVILLE, ILLINOIS, 1861
DIED IN CHICAGO, ILLINOIS, 1927

The youngest of the "Duveneck boys" Oliver Dennett Grover is most closely associated with the city of Chicago, where he enjoyed a long and prosperous career. He traveled frequently, searching out new subjects to fuel his imagination, yet he maintained a formidable presence in the windy city, and in addition to earning a comfortable living as a painter of portraits, landscapes, and still-lifes, served as either the president or founder of almost every important art organization located there.

In 1879 Grover arrived in Munich fresh from a year's study at the Chicago Academy of Design. He enrolled in drawing classes at the Royal Academy, but left the next year in order to attend Duveneck's popular school. From 1880 to 1884 he passed the winters in Florence and summers in Venice with his mentor and colleagues, and it is likely that he received rudimentary instruction in etching from his classmate Otto Bacher. After leaving Duveneck's group, Grover made his way to Paris, where he enrolled in the Académie Julian, receiving instruction from well-known academicians Gustave Boulanger, Jules Lefebvre, and Jean-Paul Laurens. Upon his return to Chicago in 1885 he accepted a teaching position at the Art Institute, which he held until 1892. From 1905 to 1907 he operated an art school in Florence, and later that decade he returned to his teaching position at the Art Institute.

Although Grover produced a small number of etchings, it is possible to trace the development of his etching skills by comparing his untitled landscape of Siena, produced during his tenure as one of the Duveneck boys, with the etching *The Lido, Venice*, created several years after he had left the group. In the former, the composition appears to have been conceived hastily; the artist's primary objective appears to have been little more than to sketch the most salient details of the Tuscan landscape, the gently rolling hills, the sparse vegetation, and a stately villa. Overall, the line work seems tentative, as though Grover was still learning how to handle the needle. In contrast, the line work in *The Lido, Venice* is more controlled, the entire composition showing greater facility with the needle. The biting and printing of the plate also show greater skill; the warm brown ink lends the print a particularly pleasing effect.

The scene depicted was an especially popular motif for artists visiting the medieval city. According to the travel writer E. V. Lucas, the Lido, a long narrow piece of land covered with yellow sand and populated with shade trees and picnic grounds, served three primary purposes; it afforded Venice protection from the assaults of the Adriatic Sea, it provided the city's inhabitants and visitors with a place for recreation, and it was a unrivaled area for bathing during the summer months.[17]

[17] E.V. Lucas, *A Wanderer in Venice* (New York: The MacMillan Co., 1914) 267-268.

SOURCES:
The Illinois Historical Art Project, Techny, Illinois.

Untitled Landscape (Siena, Italy), 1883
Etching on wove paper
150 x 270 mm
6 x 10 5/8 inches
Spencer Museum of Art, The University of
Kansas: Gift of Mr. and Mrs. E.E. Bayles,
1964.123

Entrance to the Rue de Mai, not dated
Etching on wove paper
176 x 251 mm
7 x 10 inches
Spencer Museum of Art, The University of
Kansas: Gift of Mrs. Arthur Hall in memory
of her husband, 1981.96

ARTHUR HALL

BORN IN BOWIE, TEXAS, 1889
DIED IN ALBUQUERQUE, NEW MEXICO, 1981

Although today he is most closely associated with the Prairie Print Makers, head-quartered in Lindsborg, Kansas, Arthur Hall was also a world traveler who felt comfortable in the bohemian artists' cultures of Paris and Santa Fe. He received his early training at the Art Institute of Chicago. However, his education was interrupted by America's involvement in World War I. Enlisting in the military in 1917, Hall was assigned to the infantry in southern France. While stationed there, he passed quiet moments away from the concerns of battle making drawings of his experiences, most of them pleasant scenes of village life along the Côte d'Azur.

With his war experiences behind him, Hall returned to Chicago and married Norma Bassett, whom he had met while studying at the Art Institute. The newlyweds moved to El Dorado, Kansas in 1923 so that Norma, also interested in printmaking, could accept a teaching position. Arthur found work as a court stenographer, a job that provided him with ample time to pursue his art.

The Halls took an extended trip abroad in 1925. Their first stop was the picturesque Côte d'Azur, where the couple passed many delightful days rambling about the charming hill towns of Provence. It was while on one of these excursions that they made the acquaintance of the English etcher E. S. Lumsden (1883-1948), author of *The Art of Etching* (1925), and his wife Mable Royds (1874-1941), herself an accomplished printmaker specializing in colored block prints. Finding that they had much in common, the Lumsdens persuaded the Halls to come to Scotland for study. While Arthur honed his etching skills under Lumsden's watchful eyes, Norma, encouraged by Royd's guidance, further developed her block print technique; her mature style was also influenced by Japanese *ukiyo-e* prints.

It was during their travels in the south of France that Arthur conceived *Entrance to the Rue de Mai* and *Sospel, France*. Both prints are possibly based on preliminary sketches, as this was the artist's preferred working method. *Entrance to the Rue de Mai* depicts one of the quaint corners of southern France the Halls happened upon during their wanderings. The boat laden with fish traps suggests a coastal location, perhaps one of the small fishing communities like Fréjus. The cobblestone streets and weather-beaten façades of the ancient buildings, the three elderly women engaged in lively conversation, and the laundry hanging from open windows suggest the charming character of the place.

Arthur displayed his mastery of the drypoint technique, which he acquired during his studies with Lumsden, in etchings such as *Sospel, France.* In this process, burrs produced by the etcher's needle hold ink and help to create the high range of rich tonal passages visible in the print. Located in the French Alps, medieval Sospel was once the second most important town in the county of Nice, and occupied a strategic position for many years. The Old Bridge that spans the Bavère River, the subject of Arthur's etching, once served as a tollgate on the old salt route. The salt, used to preserve food and serve the needs of cattle and of leather manufacturers, came from the marshes of Hyères and Toulon. It was unloaded in Nice and then sent northward to Turin, having to pass first through Sospel. Similar bridges have existed in this location since the 12th century. The one pictured in Arthur's etching was rebuilt in 1823, and it was virtually destroyed by German forces during World War II. Fortunately, the Old Bridge, which has long been the town's emblem, was fully restored in 1953 by the École des Beaux-Arts so that today it appears much as it did when Arthur first saw it.

Returning to the United States after their two-year European sojourn, the Halls eventually settled in Howard, Kansas and became charter members of the Prairie Print Makers, Arthur serving in the post of secretary for many years. Feeling an affinity with the American Southwest, the couple moved to Santa Fe, New Mexico in 1944, and soon became part of the artists' colony located there. In 1950 they opened an art school housed in a rural adobe villa near Alcade called the Rancho del Rio. The school closed in1957 after Norma's death.

Arthur remarried in the late 1950s and took his new wife to Spain. For unexplained reasons he ceased making etchings and turned his attention to watercolors. The Halls eventually returned to the Southwest and established a home in Albuquerque, where Arthur lived out the remainder of his life.

S o u r c e s :
Barbara Thompson O'Neill, and George C. Foreman, *The Prairie Print Makers* (Wichita, Kan.: Gallery Ellington, 1984).

Sospel, France, not dated
Etching on laid paper
213 x 250 mm
8 1/2 x 9 3/4 inches
Spencer Museum of Art, The University of
Kansas: Gift of Mrs. Arthur Hall in memory
of her husband, 1981.97

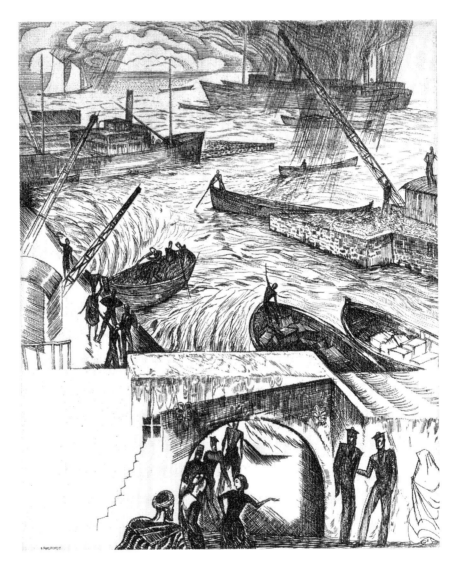

Casablanca Port, c. 1928-29
Etching on laid paper
222 x 183 mm
8 7/8 x 7 1/4 inches
Spencer Museum of Art, The University of
Kansas: Gift of Mrs. Merle Shera, 1998.51

THOMAS HANDFORTH

BORN IN TACOMA, WASHINGTON, 1897
DIED IN PASADENA, CALIFORNIA, 1948

Thomas Handforth was the quintessential artist-wanderer; his extensive travels throughout Europe and Asia, and the artistic influences to which he was exposed enriched his art. According to Handforth, his birthplace of Tacoma, Washington, an active port city with a long history of trade with Asia, was partially responsible for his lifelong interest in foreign cultures, in particular the Far East, and for his predilection for travel. Another important influence was an old two-volume book containing reproductions of Katsushika Hokusai's *One Hundred Views of Mt. Fujiyama,* [*sic*] which he had inherited from a granduncle who had traveled the globe while serving in the British Army. As the artist explained late in life, his ultimate goal as a printmaker was to recapture the spirit he discovered in Hokusai's woodblock prints.[18]

[18] Thomas Handforth, "Personal Progress Toward the Orient," *The Hornbook Magazine* Vol. XXVI (October, 19, 1950) 61-62.

Handforth's first direct contact with a foreign culture occurred in 1918 when he enlisted in World War I; he spent approximately six months in France. He returned to the United States after the war's conclusion and, having committed himself to a career in the visual arts, enrolled at the National Academy of Design and the Art Students League where he studied with Mahonri Young (1877-1957), an accomplished printmaker who likely introduced Handforth to the art of etching. Filled with a restless energy and eager to develop his skills, he returned to France late in 1919. He passed the next six years in Paris, studying at the École des Beaux-Arts, the Académie Colarossi, and the Académie de la Grand Chaumière. It was during this period that Handforth began to favor etching, a medium he thought to be particularly apropos to the vagabond artist. The stylistic differences that one finds in Handforth's early etchings like *The Shepherdess* (1922) and *Merry-Go-Round* (1922) indicate that he was experimenting with the possibilities of the medium. Whereas *The Shepherdess* is essentially a study in pure contour drawing and an early example of Handforth's effective use of open space, *Merry-Go-Round* is decidedly rococo and decorative, the composition enlivened by rich tonal variations.

While based in Paris, Handforth roamed over the European continent, visiting countries such as Austria, Hungary, and Italy, the latter providing the inspiration for the etching *The Bride Francesca*. In this etching an elegantly dressed young bride

The Bride Francesca, 1927
Etching on laid paper
237 x 175 mm
9 1/2 x 7 inches
Spencer Museum of Art, The University of
Kansas: Gift of Mrs. Merle Shera, 1998.42

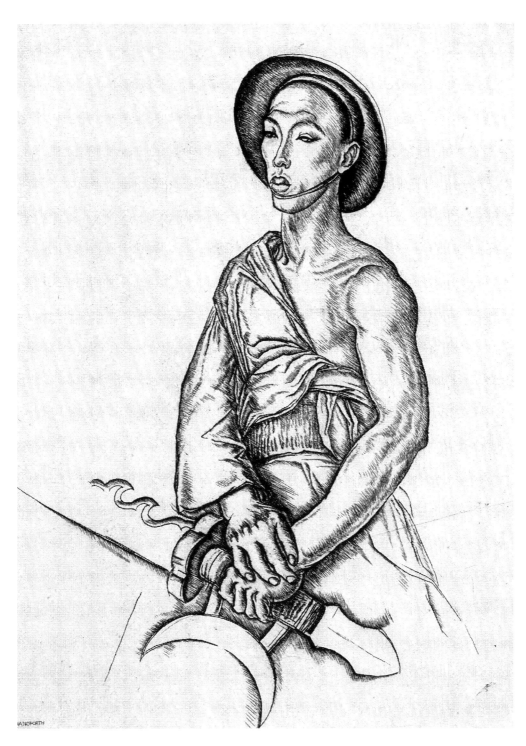

Warrior, Peiping, 1933
Etching on laid paper
235 x 180 mm
9 3/8 x 7 1/4 inches
Spencer Museum of Art, The University of
Kansas: Gift of Mrs. Merle Shera, 1988.47

adopts a classical pose in which her body is given a subtle twist; the hands lie quietly in the folds of her white gown while her gaze is directed out of the picture frame to the right. The bride sits erect, her dark soulful eyes framed by the ringlets of hair that cascade down her shoulders. In contrast to many of his colleagues who favored architectural subjects, Handforth dedicated a significant number of plates to capturing the likenesses of the people he encountered during his travels. As this print clearly shows, Handforth was a skilled and sensitive portraitist.

A brief journey to Morocco in 1928-29 produced prints like *Casablanca Port*. In this stylized rendering of an active port, Handforth used a progression of diagonal lines, seen in the large freighters hauling exotic goods, to lead the viewer through the congested harbor to the horizon. People from all walks of life and locales populate the scene. Some are occupied by daily activities while others are engaged in moments of private conversation, as in the two male figures in the foreground. Handforth's drawing is controlled and disciplined. Repetitive lines define and shape various forms, and the artist's effective use of plate tone heightens the play of light and dark.

In 1930 Handforth set out for Mexico and, inspired by Hokusai's *One Hundred Views of Mt. Fujiyama,* [sic] he began a series of etchings he intended to call *One Hundred Views of Popocatepetl.* Handforth completed less than a dozen plates before he was called back to New York to receive a Guggenheim Fellowship, which allowed him to travel to Asia. Handforth arrived in Peking, China in 1930 expecting to stay about two weeks. The journey was extended six years, during which Handforth explored China, Japan, and Mongolia. As always, his principal interests were the people and their cultural practices. *Warrior-Peiping* dates from this journey and is another example of his work in portraiture. Despite a number of anatomical irregularities like the awkward rendering of the figure's hands, his oversized wrists and small torso, the warrior's face is masterfully drawn and remarkably expressive, suggesting the subject's own sense of personal power. The ceremonial sword he holds in his hands is out of proportion and much too large for the petite warrior, but such visual disjunctions hardly lessen the impact of Handforth's prints. In China, Handforth decided to try his hand at writing and illustrating children's books based on his travels. His first literary venture, titled *Mei Li*, tells the story of a young Chinese girl he came to know while living in Peking, and for this effort Handforth was awarded the Caldecott Medal for best children's book in 1938. This success was followed a year later by *Faraway Meadow* (1939), which was inspired by the artist's trip to India in 1937.

Handforth returned to the United States in 1939 via Italy and Paris, the rumblings of World War II driving him home. He set aside his etching tools in order to concentrate on landscape painting, which took him to the Southwest. In 1942 Handforth re-enlisted in the Army, but served only six months. He passed the last four years of his life, 1944 to 1948, mostly in California, the state's scenery providing him with the subject matter for his last paintings.

SOURCES:
Louise Seaman Bechtel et al. "Thomas Handforth: Memorial Issue," *The Hornbook Magazine* Vol. XXVI (October, 19, 1950).

Le Village, Normandie, c. 1907
Etching on wove paper
135 x 213 mm
5 1/2 x 8 1/2 inches
Spencer Museum of Art, The University
of Kansas: Anonymous Gift, 1998.373

LESTER G. HORNBY

BORN IN LOWELL, MASSACHUSETTS, 1882
DIED IN ROCKPORT, MASSACHUSETTS, 1956

Whereas many of his colleagues were drawn to depict the architectural wonders of Europe, Lester Hornby exhibited a particular fondness for the people. Human beings animate his decidedly narrative prints, which convey a strong sense of unbiased observation. Hornby explored the picturesque nooks of large urban centers like Paris as well as the quaint villages of the countryside where life had remained basically unchanged for centuries. An illustrator by temperament and by profession, Hornby's prints tell simple stories about life's pleasures and sorrows.

A self-taught etcher, Hornby's earliest prints document his efforts to master the medium, as well as his travels throughout New England. While studying at the Rhode Island School of Design in the early years of the twentieth century, Hornby was awarded a traveling scholarship, and in 1906 he set sail for Paris. He began his studies at the Académie Julian with Jean-Paul Laurens, and later attended the Académie Colarossi, the Académie Delacluse, and the Académie de la Grand Chaumière. He spent breaks in classroom instruction wandering throughout Europe and North Africa; a winter voyage to Tunisia in 1908 inspired prints of storytellers, musicians, and traders.

The year before, while residing in Paris, Hornby had ventured north, and from this journey produced etchings like *Le Village, Normandie.* By this time Hornby's etching style had fully matured, his light touch with the needle firmly in place. Etchings like this demonstrate his use of the curved or looped line that became a signature characteristic of his prints. Many loose rounded lines are employed here to render the leaves in the trees, the vegetation along the path, and the billowing clouds overhead. These energetic markings also contribute a sense of atmosphere and suggest a windy day, which is characteristic of the region.

Hornby remained headquartered in Paris until World War I, when he returned to the United States. Two years later he was back in Europe working as an independent war correspondent. He accompanied American troops to the battles of Chateau-Thierry and Belleau Woods, and from these war time experiences produced thirty-seven prints. Like Kerr Eby's, haunting images of the Great War, Hornby's etchings were essentially ignored for many years afterwards. This can be attributed to the amnesia that settled over the United States following the war, as people sought to forget the recent conflict and turn their attention to domestic problems.

After the war Hornby returned to his work as an illustrator, which had provided him with an income during his years abroad. Between 1909 and 1927 he illustrated more than eighteen books, two of which, *Sunset Rock* (1924) and *Balkan Sketches* (1927), he wrote and illustrated.

S O U R C E S :

Peter Falk, *Lester G. Hornby, Painter-Etcher* (Madison, Wisc.: Sound View Press, 1984).

Frank Weitenkampf, "Hornby—An Etcher of Today," *Art and Progress* Vol. V, no. 9 (July, 1914) 313-18.

Road in the Calaudies, Corsica, 1927
Etching on Japan paper
145 x 119 mm
5 3/4 x 4 3/4 inches
Collection of Jim and Virginia Moffett

MARY HUNTOON

BORN IN TOPEKA, KANSAS, 1896
DIED IN HOYT, KANSAS, 1970

Kansas native Mary Huntoon was an inquisitive and experimental printmaker, and during her long and successful career in the graphic arts she mined the expressive possibilities of etching, engraving, and lithography.

Huntoon's art training began at Washburn College in Topeka, where she studied painting under local artist George Stone. Like many adventurous women aspiring to a career in the visual arts in the first decades of the twentieth century, she made her way to New York City and the Art Students League. Huntoon passed several years there in the classrooms of academicians Frank Vincent Du Mond and George Bridgeman before moving on to courses taught by the revolutionary Realist painter Robert Henri. Seeking to develop her skills in drawing, she enrolled in printmaking classes offered by Whistler's disciple Joseph Pennell, who was responsible for setting Huntoon on the path of a printmaker; while under Pennell's tutelage she became technically proficient in etching, drypoint, aquatint, and lithography.

In the mid-1920s, Pennell helped Huntoon secure a commission from the George Palmer Institute for a suite of images that were to illustrate Parisian daily life, and by 1926 she and her first husband, writer Charles Hoyt, were bound for Paris. Soon after their arrival, Huntoon settled into a studio located in Montparnasse; the artist's loft six flights up provided her with a commanding view of the city and its inhabitants. Although the couple had expected to stay in Paris only a few months, they remained abroad for almost five years and took advantage of this opportunity to explore other regions in Europe. Huntoon passed several productive months wandering over the picturesque and mountainous terrain of Corsica, and produced a series of canvases capturing the island's types and landscapes. She also created etchings like *Road in the Calaudies, Corsica*, in which the viewer, adopting a birds'eye view, looks down upon a meandering roadway lined with stately buildings and lush vegetation. She achieved the rich tonal contrasts through the use of aquatint, a process in which a copper plate is first coated with a powdery resin and then heated to produce a grainy surface that creates the effect of a wash when printed.

Back in Paris, Huntoon became involved with a number of progressive printmakers, among them Joseph Hecht, an etcher and engraver, who was successful in persuading Huntoon to take up the engraver's burin. She found the medium to her liking, and began to exploit the expressive possibilities of pure contour drawing. Engravings like *Momus* (1928), which relied entirely on outline, attracted immediate attention. *Momus* was named one of the 50 Best Prints of the Year by the American Institute of Graphic Arts. While residing in Paris, Huntoon also became well-acquainted with Stanley William Hayter, founder of Atelier 17, an avant-garde artists's cooperative that was dedicated to expanding the boundaries of intaglio printmaking. Paris in the late 1920s afforded many opportunities to aspiring American artists and Huntoon clearly benefited from these experiences.

Hoyt died on a visit to New York in 1928; Huntoon remained in Paris until 1930 when she returned to Topeka. Two years later she wed artist Lester T. Hull and the couple took an extended honeymoon abroad, traveling in Czechoslovakia, Italy, and Germany; Huntoon's decidedly unconventional etching *Beer House, Old Berlin*, most likely dates from this period in her life. The artist's love of drawing is readily apparent in this print, for the ramshackle beer hall and the surrounding neighborhood are rendered in lines of various widths and depths. Works like this, which rely almost entirely on the expressive properties of line, show an affinity with the type of engraving that brought Huntoon to the attention of critics.

In the late 1930s Huntoon assumed a more public role in the visual arts when she became the Director of the Federal Works of Art Project in Kansas, a program that sought to bring relief to unemployed artists in the state during the bleak years of the Great Depression. In the late 1940s Huntoon interests turned to the newly recognized field of art therapy, and in her work with mentally ill patients she became an important pioneer in the discipline. According to Huntoon, art could provide a vehicle for the expression of inner conflicts. She achieved much success in the field of art therapy and published numerous articles that explained her theories and findings. In the 1960s Huntoon settled into a period of well-earned retirement, passing away in 1970.

SOURCES:
Margaret Whittemore ed., "The Etchings of Mary Huntoon," *The Delta-Phi-Delta Palette* Vol. 10 no. 1 (December, 1929) 11-13.

Beer House, Old Berlin, c. 1925-30
Etching on laid rag paper
126 x 177 mm
5 x 7 1/6 inches
Collection of Jim and Virginia Moffett

Relics of Roviano, Italy, not dated
Etching on laid paper
203 x 160 mm
7 5/16 x 6 3/8 inches
Anonymous Loan

BERTHA E. JAQUES

BORN IN COVINGTON, OHIO, 1863
DIED IN CHICAGO, ILLINOIS, 1941

For more than three decades Bertha Jaques was the inexhaustible force behind the Chicago Society of Etchers. In addition to her responsibilities as the Society's secretary, she organized its annual exhibitions and its traveling exhibitions, and wrote extensively about the many artists associated with the organization. An accomplished etcher and printer, Jaques understood the complexities of this medium as well as any of her male counterparts and never passed up an opportunity to teach others. Her lectures, which often included live demonstrations, were very popular with the public; her popular handbook, *Concerning Etchings* (1912), was reprinted in numerous editions and also attracted a large and appreciative audience.

Jaques was one of the pioneers of etching in Chicago; her interest in the medium was kindled in the early 1890s when she and her husband Willem K. Jaques attended an exhibition of etchings at the Columbian Exposition. Shortly thereafter, Willem presented Bertha with copies of Hamerton's *Etchings and Etchers* (1868) and Koehler's translation of Lalanne's *Treatise on Etching* (1880), which she studied carefully. Willem, a respected surgeon and part-time inventor, also provided her with needles and plates, which he fabricated out of discarded materials, since no etching materials could be found in Chicago. Proofing the plates was the next obstacle to overcome. After a number of trial methods met with failure—including passing the plates through the wringer of a washing machine—Willem was able to secure a second-hand printing press in Milwaukee, which he successfully converted into an etching press; for many years it was the only etching press in Chicago. With all of the prerequisite tools and materials at her disposal, Bertha began etching subjects that were familiar to her, such as the factories along the Chicago River. She kept scrupulous records of her experiments, noting such things as the number of minutes a plate was in the bath, the strength and temperature of the acid, and the types of plates and inks used.

In 1908, Jaques traveled to Japan to visit her her close friend and fellow etcher Helen Hyde. Approximately two years later she took a grand tour of Europe and devoted a number of etchings to some of the picturesque subjects she discovered during her journey, such as the tidal marshes near London, the congested streets of Cairo, and the ancient fishing wharves of Algeciras, Portugal. In *Relics of Roviano, Italy*, Jaques depicted some of the treasures she collected during her Italian sojourn, which include an old religious book, a metal baby feeder, a ceramic vessel, swatches of lace spilling out of a small decorated box, and a piece of antique statuary, hidden in the shadows. This odd assortment of objects, organized into a pleasing arrangement, is set on top of an elaborately carved wooden chest embellished with elephant heads and a grotesque mask.

By 1924 Jaques had perfected a technique of color etching that she used to depict the things she loved most, the many flowers and plants she cultivated in her garden. She recorded their singular characteristics with botanical accuracy, which helped to make them among her most popular works.

S o u r c e s :

Joby Patterson, *Bertha E. Jaques and the Chicago Society of Etchers* (Madison, N.J.: Fairleigh Dickinson University Press, 2002).

Bertha Jaques, *Concerning Etchings* (Chicago: Chicago Society of Etchers, 1912).

Untitled Landscape, 1932
Etching on wove paper
138 x 306 mm
5 1/2 x 12 1/8 inches
Spencer Museum of Art, The University of
Kansas: Bequest of Wallace Pratt, 1982.18

Donald Shaw MacLaughlan

Born in Charlottetown, Canada, 1876
Died in Marrakech, Morocco, 1938

Donald Shaw MacLaughlan began etching at the age of twenty-three while studying in Paris. Believing it to be the instrument best suited to his personal vision, he dedicated the remainder of his life to exploiting the expressive possibilities of the medium. Critics at the turn of the twentieth century were unanimous in their praise of his work, citing his sincere vision and honest craftsmanship as the chief hallmarks of his work.

Born and raised on a family farm on Prince Edward Island, MacLaughlan was still in his teens when his parents decided to move to Boston in 1890. Shortly after settling there, he began attending an art school run by W. D. Hamilton. Approximately eight years later, MacLaughlan was attending classes at the École des Beaux-Arts in Paris, studying with Jean-Léon Gérôme and Jean-Paul Laurens. After a brief trip to Italy the following year, he returned to Paris intent on becoming an etcher, and by 1901 two of his prints had been accepted by the Salon de la Société Nationale des Beaux-Arts; MacLaughlan was elected an Associate of this august institution two years later in 1903.

The etchings of Whistler, Lepère, and Haden were MacLaughlan's primary textbooks. He studied their disparate techniques carefully, his own approach to the medium developing out of their lessons. While living in Paris, MacLaughlan was befriended by another American expatriate, Herman Armour Webster, himself an aspiring etcher. The two men formed a close professional relationship, as can be seen from their early works, which share many affinities in technique and subject matter. Like Webster, MacLaughlan produced numerous landscapes, village, and city scenes derived from his travels in France, Italy, and England.

Early in his career MacLaughlan sought out the picturesque in the old quarters of Paris, finding his inspiration in the narrow cobblestone streets untouched by Haussmannization. It was the character of the crumbling medieval buildings and the people who resided in them that captured his imagination, as seen in *Quartier des Gobelins*, in which neighbors gossip through open windows and linen hangs out to dry. MacLaughlan always worked directly on the grounded plate with the needle, every line having been previously arranged in his mind. In works like this he achieved gradations in tone by liberal stopping out, a common practice at the time. In later years he began using nitric acid, drawing and etching alternately, this technique giving a greater freedom and spontaneity to his works. Few etchers bestowed such care or labor on printing as MacLaughlan did, for among other things he chose to grind and prepare his own inks, realizing that some plates required a stiffer ink than others. He also took great care in his choice of papers, and like many of his contemporaries he scoured Europe for old Italian paper of 16th and 17th centuries for his etchings, which were generally issued in small editions.

By 1909 MacLaughlan was in Venice, a city that inspired him to produce some of his most remarkable works. He settled in Asolo, Giorgione's country, until the cataclysm wrought by the World War forced him to flee. He sought temporary refuge in Spain, and later in England, where he produced a series of etchings depicting the Cornish landscape; the Spencer's *Untitled Landscape* is surely related to this group. In these etchings from the end of MacLaughlan's career all is light and airy. A sense of peace characterizes these Arcadian landscapes in which calm rounded trees are stirred by a gentle wind and the homesteads are separated by the graceful lines of sloping hedgerows, stone walls, and rail fences.

S O U R C E S:

Marie Bruette, *Descriptive Catalogue of the Etched Work of Donald Shaw MacLaughlan* (Chicago: Albert Roullier Art Galleries, 1924).

James Laver, "The Etchings of Donald Shaw MacLaughlan," *Print Collector's Quarterly* Vol. 13 (December, 1924) 322-344.

Quartier des Gobelins, 1901
Etching on wove paper
252 x 163 mm
9 7/8 x 6 3/8 inches
Anonymous Loan

Cathedral, Laon, I, 1906
Etching on Japan paper
220 x 137 mm
8 5/8 x 5 3/8 inches
Spencer Museum of Art, The University of
Kansas: Museum purchase, Peter T. Bohan
Art Acquisition Fund, 1992.125

John Marin

BORN IN RUTHERFORD, NEW JERSEY, 1872
DIED IN CAPE SPLITZ, MAINE, 1953

At the time he embarked on his first journey to Europe in 1905, John Marin was an artist in search of direction; two years of study at the Pennsylvania Academy of the Fine Arts with Thomas Anshutz (1851-1912) and William Merritt Chase and a year at the Art Students League in New York with Frank DuMond (1865-1951) had yielded unsatisfactory results. Buoyed by his father's encouragement and promise of financial support, Marin set out for Paris with renewed determination. Among the items in his baggage were Maxime Lalanne's *Treatise on Etching* (1866) and a volume devoted to Rembrandt's etchings written by Charles Blanc (1859).

When he arrived in Paris on September 27, Marin was met by his younger step-brother, Charles Bittinger, himself an aspiring artist. In a fortuitous twist of fate Bittinger had recently renounced his interest in etching; aware of Marin's growing appreciation for the art, he graciously provided his sibling with all of the requisite materials, including needles, copper plates, and an etching press. With these tools and the etching manuals he had carried across the ocean, Marin set to work mastering the medium, and by the the end of the year he had produced twelve plates with varying degrees of success.

Early in 1906, Marin traveled to Amsterdam and passed several months there honing his etching skills. He returned to Paris by way of Laon, staying long enough to produce nine etchings of the picturesque medieval town, most of these works depicting some element of the city's magnificent fifteenth-century cathedral. *Cathedral, Laon, I* is the only print in this series to have been published in an edition, all of the others are known only through two or three proofs.

Heavily influenced by impressionist art theory, Marin sought in his etchings to capture the spontaneous and intuitive impression of a scene, and in order to achieve this objective, he drew directly on the plate without the aid of a preparatory drawing or sketch. A consummate craftsman, Marin was involved in all matters of production. He carefully etched, inked, and printed his own plates, his standards exceedingly high. A rather furtive artist, he preferred to remain aloof when working, and like a good many of his contemporaries who favored architectural subjects, Marin spent a great deal of time searching for an original viewpoint to record.

In this work the viewer gazes across a small square courtyard, a tower of the great church rising over the rooftop of the adjacent building. Marin's nervous roving lines—a signature characteristic of his etchings—are used to articulate such elements as the tiles covering the mansard roof and the delicate tracery of the cathedral's imposing tower, the expressive line work lending a sense of immediacy and vitality to the composition. Shadows are suggested by areas of delicate cross-hatching and abstract patterns composed of deeply etched vertical lines. Marin's use of *retroussage*, or selective wiping, heightens the play of light and dark. As in many his early etchings, human beings are little more than *staffage*, their presence barely articulated, as in the ghost-like figure ascending the steps at the left.

During his extended trip abroad, from 1905-1910, Marin produced more than one hundred plates, with subjects derived from his travels to Rome, Florence, Venice, Bruges, Antwerp, and Brussels. Although he would continue to produce etchings for the remainder of his career, Marin's interest turned to watercolors upon his return to the United States in 1911, and it is for these that he is best known today.

S o u r c e s :

Carl Zigrosser, *The Complete Etchings of John Marin Catalogue Raissoné* (Philadelphia: Philadelphia Museum of Fine Art, 1969).

Untitled (Landscape), 1883
Etching on wove paper
150 x 215 mm
6 x 8 5/8 inches
Spencer Museum of Art, The University of
Kansas: Gift of Mr. and Mrs. E.E. Bayles,
1964.118

Charles E. Mills

BORN IN PITTSBURGH, PENNSYLVANIA, 1856
DIED IN DEDHAM, MASSACHUSETTS, 1956

Little is known of Charles Mills' early life. He surfaces in the history of art as one of Frank Duveneck's less known students, which is surprising given that he studied with Duveneck in Europe for approximately ten years. When Mills returned to the United States in the mid-1880s he settled in Boston, where he opened a studio and established himself as a portraitist, muralist, and designer of stained glass windows; one of his best known commissions is a suite of windows for Trinity Church in Copley Square. In later years he turned to painting landscapes *en plein air*, adopting a loose impressionist technique that featured a bright palette and feathery brushstrokes. In spite of his apparent success, records show that Mills exhibited his works infrequently at the Boston Art Club in 1884 and 1885 and the Art Institute of Chicago in 1891.

Although Mills is listed as a painter in the records, the untitled prints in the Spencer's collection indicate that he also tried his hand at etching while he was a member of Duveneck's circle; both works are signed and inscribed by the artist "Florence, 1883." It is also likely that both plates were printed there and issued in small editions. The first work depicts an area in the Tuscan hills, perhaps somewhere near Florence, since several stately villas dominate the landscape. The large dark villa in the foreground, worked over vigorously with the etching needle, is rendered in a loose spontaneous manner, those in the background are defined by a few hastily drawn outlines. The sketch-like quality of the drawing shows an affinity with that practiced by his teacher and fellow students, all of them favoring a loose and rapid drawing technique.

The subject of Mills' untitled Venetian scene is the Grand Canal, the elegant gondolas that glide across its surface, and the ancient palazzos that line its banks. The large structure to the left in the background is the Palazzo Balbi; the campanile of Santa Maria Gloriosa dei Frari rises above its rooftop to the right. The sixteenth-

AMERICAN ETCHERS ABROAD   107

century Palazzo Balbi, with its sixteenth-century classicizing façade, is attributed to the great Venitian architect and sculptor Alessandro Vittoria (1525-1608).

Untitled (Venice), 1883
Etching on wove paper
95 x 135 mm
3 7/8 x 5 1/2 inches
Spencer Museum of Art, The University of
Kansas: Gift of Mr. and Mrs. E.E. Bayles,
1964.129

Cours des Halles, c. 1908-10
Etching on parchment
300 x 245 mm
11 7/8 x 9 3/4 inches
Collection of Jim and Virginia Moffett

B. J. O. (Bror Julius Olsson) Nordfeldt

Born in Skane, Sweden, 1878
Died in Henderson, Texas, 1955

In the opening decades of the twentieth century, B. J. O. Nordfeldt was considered a master etcher. At a time when his highly individualistic paintings attracted few buyers, he was able to derive a comfortable living from the sale of his etchings. His romantic renderings of a city's architecture, as in *Cours des Halles*, garnered significant attention from critics and received several prestigious awards. Nordfeldt's contribution to this medium has attracted little scholarly attention since, the etchings having been overshadowed by his adventurous and independent approach to painting and his modernist woodblock prints.

Exactly when and where Nordfeldt first picked up the copper plate and etching needle is unknown. Born in Sweden, he was thirteen when his family emigrated to the United States and settled in Chicago. He began his formal art education at the Art Institute of Chicago in 1897, and by 1900 he was working abroad. A self-described radical, Nordfeldt eschewed academic instruction in favor of charting his own course as a painter. He opened his own studio soon after arriving in Paris, and there set out to assimilate the modernist developments he encountered into his own style, a process that took many years. Nordfeldt acquired his woodblock printing skills in London under the tutelage of Frank Morley Fletcher (1866-1949), who was one of the leading practitioners of Japanese woodblock printing in the West. Nordfeldt's interest in woodblock prints is confined to two inventive phases, from 1900 to 1906, and from 1915 to 1917, after which he abandoned the medium entirely. In 1907 he set aside the woodblock prints temporarily in order to concentrate on painting and etching.

From 1908 to 1910, Nordfeldt wandered through Europe, spending most of his time in London, Paris, Florence, and his native Sweden. One of his main reasons for going abroad at this time was to create a series of etchings for *Harper's* magazine, which had commissioned him to create a series of illustrations for travel articles written by Emery Potter and Mary Heaton Vorse. *Cours des Halles* was created during this sojourn, and may well be connected to this commission. It is a fine example of Nordfeldt's rather conservative approach to etching, which becomes more apparent when one compares his work in this medium to either his avant-garde paintings or his modernist woodblock prints. A consummate craftsman in the art of etching, Nordfeldt could often be found roaming the congested streets with a coated copper plate tucked safely into his pocket. He eschewed preliminary sketches, preferring to draw directly on the plate; he was especially skilled in the use of the line, which may begin faintly and deepen significantly in a single stroke. Nordfeldt also insisted on pulling every impression himself, the editions of his etchings often ranging from fifteen to twenty-five prints. Between 1910 and 1925, when he abandoned etching entirely in order to devote his full attention to painting, sales of his prints constituted the major portion of Nordfeldt's annual income.

Although painting became his primary concern, he experimented briefly with lithography in the mid-1930s, learning the rudiments of the medium in Wichita, Kansas, from William Dickerson (1904-1972). Nordfeldt eventually settled in Lambertville, New Jersey, and there devoted the last ten years of his life to painting.

S O U R C E S :

Fiona Donavan et al. *The Woodblock Prints of B. J. O. Nordfeldt: A Catalogue Raisonné* (Minneapolis: University Art Museum, University of Minnesota, 1991).

Van Deren Coke, *Nordfeldt the Painter* (Albuquerque: University of New Mexico Press, 1972).

Venetian Church by Moonlight, 1930s
Etching on wove paper
275 mm x 217 mm
10 7/8 x 8 1/2 inches
Promised Gift

LAWTON PARKER

BORN IN FAIRFIELD, MICHIGAN, 1868
DIED IN PASADENA, CALIFORNIA, 1954

Lawton Parker's approach to etching was decidedly unconventional and highly experimental. He became interested in the graphic arts late in life, after he had achieved considerable success as a painter; in 1913 he was the first American to be awarded a gold medal at the Paris Salon for his painting *La Paresse (Idleness)*, which can be described as a *mélange* of his academic training, impressionist painting technique, and symbolist sensibility.

An influential mediator between the art worlds of Paris and Chicago, Parker spent much of his career crossing the Atlantic. In the 1920s he acquired the Château d'Andecy at Plailly, in Oise, located approximately twenty miles south of Paris. By this time critical interest in his oil painting had waned considerably—his favorite motif of the female nude had fallen out of fashion—and Parker began to focus his attentions on producing etchings, drawings, and watercolors. He was forced to flee France with the outbreak of World War II, and upon his return to the United States he settled in Pasadena, California, where he carried on his graphic experiments with little notice until shortly before his death in 1954.

Although he kept detailed records of his experiments, Parker's approach to etching is still not fully understood and thus awaits further study. He worked with highly unconventional materials, such as celluloid, a type of plastic that resembles mylar, which he preferred over the more traditional copper plate. *Venetian Church by Moonlight* is a fine example of Parker's etching technique. Like many of his prints, this evocative night-time scene began as a dry-point etching, the most basic lines of the composition rendered with an etching needle; in some instances additional elements, like architectural details and figures, may also be scratched into the celluloid. It is thought that the tonal variations found in works like this, which give the prints a decidedly painterly effect, were achieved through a monotype-like process or some related technique.

Working with celluloid had some advantages; for example, it eliminated the need of biting the plate. Once the drawing had been completed—Parker's finished prints were generally achieved through progressive states—the plate would be inked with the scratched marks holding the ink. The plate was then covered with a piece of fine paper and cranked through either a lithographic or etching press under moderate pressure for printing. Great care had to be taken at this stage of the process since celluloid is highly explosive substance when under pressure.

Parker is known for reworking many of his etchings after printing. On some occasions he would clarify details with the point of a pencil, at other times he would darken a shadow with either a piece of charcoal or ink laid on with a fine brush; white gouache was often used to emphasize certain highlights. Sometimes an etching was so thoroughly reworked that all references to the printing technique were obliterated. The experimental nature that is so characteristic of Parker's etchings is part of their attraction, for they encourage the viewer to look beyond the surface and explore the manner in which they were created.

SOURCES:
Richard H. Love and Danny Miller, *Lawton Parker, 1868-1954: Works on Paper* (Chicago: Haase-Mumm Publishing Company, Inc., 1995).

Auberge du Cheval Blanc, 1902
Etching on wove paper
249 x 196 mm
10 x 7 3/4 inches
Spencer Museum of Art, The University of
Kansas: Gift of Bud and Ruby Jennings,
Prairie Print Makers Collection, 1991.373

Orville Houghton Peets

BORN IN CLEVELAND, OHIO, 1884
DIED IN LEWES, DELAWARE, 1968

Highly regarded as a portraitist and etcher during his lifetime, the classically trained Orville Houghton Peets is little known today, due in part to his commitment to a conservative academic style that was displaced by the advent of modernism. His father, Edward O. Peets, a poet, illustrator, and part-time portrait painter, guided his son towards a career in the visual arts. The younger Peets took to illustration, and while still in his teens created political cartoons for his hometown newspaper, *The Cleveland Leader*. Learning of his precocious talents, a relative living in England offered to pay for his training abroad, an offer Peets could hardly turn down.

Peets arrived in Paris shortly after the turn of the twentieth century. He received his artistic training at the Académie Julian and the École des Beaux-Arts, and studied in the ateliers of Jean-Léon Gérôme, Jean-Paul Laurens, William-Adolphe Bouguereau, and Léon Bonnat. Although proud of his academic education, which stressed the importance of technique and craftsmanship with an emphasis on drawing, Peets claimed in later years that he had been more influenced by the work of his fellow students and the heady artistic milieu of Paris than by his learned professors.[19]

[19] Carol A. Nathanson, "Orville Houghton Peets: Painter, Printmaker, and Illustrator," *The American Art Journal* (Autumn, 1882) 67-8.

Exactly when Peets began to etch is unknown. However, he was producing etchings shortly after his arrival in Paris; *Auberge du Cheval Blanc* (1902) is among his earliest works. Like other etchers of his generation, Peets was heavily influenced by Whistler. He was especially fortunate in that he shared a studio with Cecil Lawson, Whistler's nephew by marriage. Lawson had served as Whistler's dealer in Paris and his apartment was filled with his etchings, which Peets was free to examine closely. However, his mature etching style has more in common with Whistler's early realist etchings, such as *The Unsafe Tenement*, than with his later and more suggestive works, like *The Garden*. In *Auberge du Cheval Blanc* Peets constructed a charming vignette in which the viewer visually eavesdrops on a man and two women engaged in conversation; perhaps they are all boarders at the hotel, returning from a long day of sightseeing. The placement of every line is given thoughtful consideration, revealing his academic training. Peets is perhaps most effective in suggesting the effects of light as it washes over the old shingled roof and the worn façade of the building, as well as the way in which it is obscured in the darkened alleyway to the right.

Peets returned to Cleveland around 1907. While he continued to produce etchings, he supported himself mainly through portraiture. Although he became quite successful, he missed the artistic milieu of Paris and returned for short trips in 1910 and 1912. In 1914 he married a former student, Ethel Canby, but soon after their wedding Peets opened another studio in Paris, having received a commission from the Century Club to create illustrations for an article on the medieval town of Senlis. While his wife waited out the war in Woodstock, New York, where they hoped to settle one day, Peets taught etching in Paris and Senlis. In 1920 he was awarded a commission from The Hispanic Society of America to produce a series of prints on Portugal, making four trips there between 1920 and 1924. Peets was especially proud of the colored etchings he produced during this time, but they never really found an appreciative audience. As Carol Nathanson reports, many of the leading theorists of the time, such as E. S. Lumsden and Joseph Pennell, believed that colored lines do not carry the same visual impact as black lines.[20]

[20] Nathanson, 74 and note 20.

Although he was reluctant to leave the advantageous working conditions he found abroad, Peets accepted a teaching position in Woodstock, New York. However, he found the dogmatic nationalism of his American colleagues irritating and stifling. He resigned and accepted a teaching post at the Wilmington Academy of Art in Delaware, where he taught painting and drawing during the day, and in the evenings a class in etching free of charge to students. In the 1940s his interests shifted to art conservation and restoration. At the same time, Peets was inundated with commissions for portraits, and his work in these two areas left him little time for anything else.

S O U R C E S :

Carol A. Nathanson, "Orville Houghton Peets: Painter, Printmaker, and Illustrator," *The American Art Journal* (Autumn, 1982) 66-80.

St. Martin's Bridge, Toledo, c. 1904
Etching on wove paper
197 x 248 mm
7 7/8 x 9 7/8 inches
Spencer Museum of Art, The University
of Kansas, 00.799

JOSEPH PENNELL

BORN IN PHILADELPHIA, PENNSYLVANIA, 1860
DIED IN BROOKLYN HEIGHTS, NEW YORK, 1926

Although Joseph Pennell belongs to the first generation of American etchers to go abroad, he greatly influenced many printmakers of the second generation, who came to know him through his prints, writings, and influential role as a teacher at the Art Students League from 1922 to 1926. Printmakers such as Mary Huntoon, received early instruction in the graphic arts from Pennell and, like many of his other students, she was profoundly effected by his passion for prints and printmaking.

Pennell committed himself to a career in the visual arts at an early age and during his teens attended the Pennsylvania School of Industrial Art and the Pennsylvania Academy of the Fine Arts. In the late 1870s he learned the rudiments of etching from Stephen Ferris (1835-1915), who had found success as a reproductive printmaker. Pennell opened a studio in Philadelphia in 1880 and supported himself by producing prints of well-known buildings for a variety of publications.

Pennell traveled to Italy on an assignment in 1883. Expecting to stay only a few months, he remained abroad for more than thirty years, excluding a few brief trips he made to New York in the early 1900s. One of Pennell's first stops in Italy was the city of Florence. Perhaps best known as the birthplace of the Italian Renaissance, the medieval city for centuries had lured aspiring artists, who came to examine and learn from the works of the great masters, painters and sculptors like Lorenzo Ghiberti, Sandro Botticelli, Leonardo da Vinci, and Michelangelo Buonaroti. Pennell's etching *The Ponte Vecchio* was created soon after his arrival in Florence, and serves as a fine example of his early etching style. Spanning the temperamental Arno River, the Ponte Vecchio is the oldest surviving bridge in the city —it was the only bridge in Florence to escape destruction in World War II. The Ponte Vecchio was constructed in 1345, and it became the preferred location of the city's blacksmiths, butchers, and tanners, all of whom used the river as a place for disposing waste. In time an incredible stench began to rise up from the Arno and in 1593, the tradesmen were evicted from their shops by Duke Ferdinand I, their empty spaces taken over by the city's prosperous goldsmiths and jewelers, who still reside there today. Something resembling a realist sensibility characterizes Pennell's depiction of the Ponte Vecchio, for he demonstrated a concern for capturing the salient details of the bridge and the buildings that lie on the opposite bank of the river. Pennell also sought to record the effects of light with accuracy, the masterful interplay of light and dark contributing to the almost palpable atmosphere.

Pennell's etching style underwent a noticeable change the following year when he moved to London and entered the orbit of James Abbott McNeill Whistler. He became one of Whistler's closest confidants and most devoted followers, and Pennell carried his mentor's teachings into the next century not only in his graphic art, but also in his writings, publications such as *The Whistler Journal* (1921) and *Etchers and Etching* (1919). Whistler's influence can be discerned in Pennell's *St. Martin's Bridge, Toledo*, and *South Door, Beauvais*. In the former etching, the fourteenth-century bridge that spans the Rio Tajo, the walled medieval city of Toledo, and lush landscape beyond have all been rendered in an abbreviated manner; the monastery of San Juan de Los Reyes and other architectural landmarks located on the opposite shore are defined by simple outlines. Working from nature as Whistler had instructed, Pennell sought to capture the first fleeting impression of the scene before him in an autographic manner by depositing his own sensations directly on the copper plate. Like his friend and mentor, Pennell exhibited a particular fondness for old papers and warm brown inks, which he generally used for his prints. And following Whistler's lead, he also printed his own plates, having acquired an etching press while living in London.

South Door, Beauvais, is one of Pennell's most Whistlerian compositions. Rather than depict the entire structure or its more famous north door as his contemporaries Ernest Roth, Jules Andre Smith, and Samuel Chamberlain were to do, Pennell, once again borrowing from Whistler, centralized the motif, and focused his attention on the cathedral's less impressive, though still magnificent, south portal. Details of the sculptural program decorating the doorway are only suggested, and the surrounding architecture dissolves as one moves out from the center. In this print a portion of the building stands in for the whole, with the cathedral, a culmination of the high gothic style, animated by the comings and goings of the people on the street outside. For this etching Pennell dispensed with the traditional acid bath. The puddling effect visible in the print indicates that he moved the acid carefully over the surface of the plate, possibly with a feather as Whistler was known to do, for his lines have become less harsh, and the range of tones significantly greater.

Pennell's European wanderings came to a close in 1917 when World War I erupted on the continent. Upon his return to the United States he began to champion lithography, having been introduced to the possibilities of the medium while under Whistler's tutelage. Lithography had undergone a recent and popular revival in Europe and when he returned to the United States, Pennell brought news of lithography's renaissance with him. Between 1904 and 1905 he produced an important series of eighteen lithographs depicting the New York skyline, and in 1922 he established the first organized classes in lithography at the Art Students League in New York. The classes attracted scores of aspiring printmakers.

Ponte Vecchio, 1883
Etching on laid paper
247 x 202 mm
9 3/4 x 7 15/16 inches
Anonymous Loan

S o u r c e s :

Joseph Pennell and Elizabeth Robins Pennell, *The Whistler Journal* (Philadelphia: J. B. Lippincott Company, 1921).

Joseph Pennell, *Etchers and Etchings* (New York: The Macmillan Company, 1919).

South Door, Beauvais, 1907
Etching on laid paper
279 x 203 mm
11 1/16 x 8 1/8 inches
Spencer Museum of Art, The University of
Kansas: Museum purchase, Letha Churchill
Walker Memorial Fund, 2003.5.1

Rue de Mont Genis, Montmartre, 1884
Etching on wove paper
138 x 212 mm
5 7/16 x 8 3/8 inches
Spencer Museum of Art, The University of
Kansas, 00.484

CHARLES ADAMS PLATT

BORN IN NEW YORK, NEW YORK, 1861
DIED IN CORNISH, NEW HAMPSHIRE, 1933

Born to a socially prominent and wealthy family in New York City, Charles Platt could have enjoyed a life of leisure but, being of an independent mind, he chose to make a name for himself in the arts. During the 1880s Platt was one of the most innovative and respected artists of the etching revival, yet in the early 1890s his interests turned to architecture, and today he is best known as the designer of the Freer Art Gallery and the National Gallery of Art in Washington, D. C. According to the influential art critic Royal Cortissoz, what set Platt apart from his contemporaries was the fact that he was "an architect who was an artist."[21]

[21] Royal Cortissoz, quoted in Van Buren, 102.

Platt began his art training in 1879, enrolling at the Art Students League and the National Academy of Design in New York. In 1880 he met Stephen Parrish (1846-1939), who became his etching instructor. For two years, Platt passed the summer months etching with Parrish on Cape Ann, Massachusetts. Their work from this time shows that both men favored views of quiet bays and harbors, each of them devoting numerous plates to the picturesque fishing wharves lined with shanties they encountered in the region.

Except for the summer of 1885, which he spent in New York City, Platt studied in Europe from 1882 to 1889. While attending the painting classes of Gustave Boulanger and Jules Lefebvre at the Académie Julian, he also found time to explore the Low Countries, Spain, and Italy, documenting his travels with the etcher's needle. The etching *Rue de Mont Genis, Montmartre*, was inspired by Platt's time in Paris. The steep *butte* or hill of Montmartre has been a mecca for artists, writers, and poets for over 200 years, its decadent and raucous bars, cabarets, and bordellos inspiring such artists as Auguste Renoir, Pablo Picasso, and Henri Toulouse-Lautrec. The heavily shaded street depicted in Platt's etching is located in the heart of Montmartre, approximately one block west of the church of Sacré-Coeur. This magnificent edifice, a pastiche of diverse artistic influences, was still under construction during Platt's visit; begun in 1870, the building was not completed until 1914.

Etchings like *Rue de Mont Genis, Montmartre*, attest to the radical change that occurred in Platt's etching style while he was abroad. The straightforward realism that characterizes his early work with Parrish was supplanted by a decidedly Whistlerian approach, in which he intentionally suppressed insignificant details and used sketchy, vigorously drawn lines to define and shape forms. The remarkable contrast of light and dark relies almost entirely on the quality of line. Deeply scored and bitten lines define elements such as the tree at the left and buildings in the distance. Platt employed fainter, lightly drawn lines like those in the sky to suggest the atmospheric effects he encountered in nature and sought to reproduce in his etchings. Tonal contrasts were further enhanced by a wash-like effect that Platt developed, which he once described as "acid tint." Human beings rarely appear in Platt's prints and when they are represented, as in this etching, they receive minimal attention.

Like others of his generation, Platt was drawn to the Netherlands, the quiet harbors he encountered in places like Dordrecht satisfying his love for views of slumbering ports. Situated between two mighty rivers, the Noord and Merwerde, which come together at the Oude Maas, Dordrecht was once an important maritime city, its historic streets attracting painters such as Nicholaes Maes, Aelbert Cuyp, and Vincent van Gogh. Platt created several etchings during his visit to Dordrecht, most of them depicting some aspect of the city's architecture as seen from the water. *Dordrecht on the Maas*, is one of his best known prints from this journey and, like Robert Swain Gifford's *Scheveningen*, it is printed on satin. As in Gifford's etching, the shimmering effects of the support complement the scene represented. In Dordrecht, Platt further simplified his compositions; the merchants' houses and *Grote Kerk* (Great Church) seen here, have been reduced to their most salient elements. Platt's dream-like images of this once vital port city have much in common with Whistler's etchings of Venice created just a few years earlier.

While traveling in Europe Platt became deeply interested in architecture and landscape design, and shortly after his return to the United States in 1889 he abandoned painting and etching in order to pursue a career as an architect. He settled in the art colony of Cornish, New Hampshire, which was an invigorating atmosphere for anyone involved in the visual, literary, and performing arts. Although Platt returned to etching sporadically after finding success as an architect, his days as an etcher were essentially over, the plates providing him with a pleasant diversion from his nine-to-five architectural practice.

S o u r c e s :
Deborah Van Buren, *A Circle of Friends* (Concord, N.H.: University of New Hampshire Press, 1985).

Exhibition Catalogue of the Works of Charles Adams Platt at the American Academy of Arts and Letters (New York: American Academy of Arts and Letters, 1938).

Dordrecht on the Maas, c. 1882-89
Etching on satin
100 x 142 mm
4 x 5 7/8 inches
Spencer Museum of Art, The University of
Kansas, 00.495

Town Square (Italy), 1883
Etching and drypoint on laid paper
212 x 311 mm
8 3/8 x 12 1/4 inches
Spencer Museum of Art, The University of
Kansas: Gift of Mr. and Mrs. E.E. Bayles,
1964.128

Julius Rolshoven

Born in Detroit, Michigan, 1858
Died in New York, New York, 1930

The son of a Detroit jeweler, Julius Rolshoven began his artistic training at the Cooper Union Art School in New York and, like many other American artists of the nineteenth century, he soon felt the need to go abroad for further instruction. He studied briefly at the Düsseldorf Academy under Hugo Crola before heading to Munich, where he came under the influence of Frank Duveneck. One of Duveneck's favorite pupils, Rolshoven was chosen to paint Duveneck's portrait for the National Academy of Design in New York.

Like Cassatt and Whistler, Rolshoven chose the life of an expatriate, but instead of living in Paris or London, he cast his lot with Italy, the decision no doubt influenced by his experiences as one of "Duveneck's Boys." After leaving Duveneck's circle Rolshoven moved to Paris and continued his studies at the Académie Julian under the tutelage of William-Adolphe Bouguereau and Tony Robert-Fleury; by 1889 he was teaching an international group of students in the art capital. In 1896 he accepted a teaching position in London but moved to Florence the following year after his wife's death. Aside from his many sojourns, which took him to such exotic locales as Tunisia and Algeria, Rolshoven remained in Italy until the outbreak of World War I. Fascinated by the American Southwest and its indigenous peoples, Rolshoven passed the war years in Santa Fe, New Mexico; along with Marsden Hartley, John Sloan, Oscar Blumenschein, and others, he helped to establish the Southwestern regional art movement. At the conclusion of the war Rolshoven returned to Italy accompanied by his new bride, Harriette Blazo. The couple purchased a thirteenth-century Florentine villa called the Castello del Diavolo, which Rolshoven would call home for the remainder of his life.

A painter by profession, Rolshoven had a short-lived interest in etching that appears to have been confined to his time in Italy as one of Duveneck's students. Only a few of his etchings have come to light; among the best known of these is *Town Square, Italy*. The print's central focus is the corner of a public square, with markets such as the Degli Fredi open for business. Nothing is known of Rolshoven's working methods beyond what can be discerned from the works themselves. In this print Rolshoven employed a compositional format first introduced by Whistler and adopted by many of his followers in which forms become less finished as one moves out from the center, as exemplified by the ghostly image of a man and his cart at the left. Other figures mill about the square; two figures in the foreground, one possibly carrying a market basket, are engaged in a lively conversation. The use of drypoint and selective wiping, which include both *retroussage* and plate tone, create rich tonal variations while also providing a clear sense of atmosphere. The suggestion of sunlight raking over a building's façade is achieved by scraping away some of the ink before printing, as seen near the top of the image where the tool marks are clearly visible.

Although Florence was Rolshoven's adopted home for over forty years, he returned to the Southwest frequently, spending the summer months in Santa Fe, which he considered his second home. A prolific painter specializing in portraiture and figure paintings, Rolshoven died in New York City in 1930, having taken ill on his last transatlantic voyage.

S O U R C E S :
Anniversary Memorial Exhibition, Julius Rolshoven, introduction by Reginald Fisher, (Santa Fe, N. M.: Museum of New Mexico Art Gallery, 1954).

The Great Bazaar, Constantinople, 1927
Etching and drypoint on wove paper
176 x 250 mm
7 x 9 7/8 inches
Spencer Museum of Art, The University of
Kansas: Gift of Bud and Ruby Jennings,
Prairie Print Makers Collection, 1991.385

LOUIS CONRAD ROSENBERG

BORN IN PORTLAND, OREGON, 1890
DIED IN PORTLAND, OREGON, 1983

Louis Rosenberg's work as an etcher spanned fewer than twenty years and yet he produced many fine etchings that document not only his life-long interest in architecture, but also his travels to faraway places. At the age of sixteen Rosenberg began a two-year apprenticeship with an architectural firm owned by T. Chapell Brown. His precocious talents were recognized early and he was awarded a scholarship from the Architecture Club of Portland, Oregon, which allowed him to further his studies in architecture at the Massachusetts Institute of Technology, where he graduated in 1914. Rosenberg was awarded an M. I. T. Traveling Fellowship the same year, but plans to study abroad had to be postponed due to the eruption of war in Europe. When the United States entered the war in 1917, Rosenberg enlisted in the Army and was stationed in the north of France, serving in the Camouflage Corps, 40th Engineers. He returned to Portland after his tour of duty in 1919, wed Marie Louise Allen, and accepted a temporary teaching position in architectural design at the University of Oregon.

The rebuilding of Europe began in the early 1920s and Rosenberg thought it an ideal time to explore the war-ravaged continent. Funded by the M. I. T. fellowship he had received six years earlier, Rosenberg traveled throughout Great Britain, western and eastern Europe, and North Africa. He enrolled in the American Academy in Rome in 1921, and there received his first instructions in the art of etching from Robert Fulton Logan (1889-1959). Rosenberg found etching to be an ideal medium for expressing his artistic interest in architectural subjects. A fast learner, he soon developed a master's sensibility for the art. By 1924 his prints were attracting notice and Rosenberg became acquainted with the English printmaker Muirhead Bone (1876-1953), who persuaded him to set aside his architectural interests temporarily in order to concentrate on etching.

Following Bone's advice, Rosenberg entered the Royal College of Art in London, where he studied for a year under the master printmaker Malcolm Osborne (1880-1963) and became technically proficient in drypoint and etching. His studies behind him, Rosenberg set out to explore the European continent and produced etchings like *Rue de Chartres, St. Malo*, also known as *La Pomme d'Or*. As in most of Rosenberg's etchings, the buildings of this quaint fishing village located on the Normandy coast are animated by the characters in the foreground, which are shown going about their daily business. The sunlight pouring over the timeworn façades suggests some familiarity with the etchings of Charles Meryon. No traces of the recent hostilities can be found; the town appears to have escaped the war unscathed.

Rosenberg's architectural interests are also manifested in works like *Aurelian Wall, Rome*. Like many of his contemporaries, he sought out ancient buildings and structures that spoke of the distant past. This massive fortress, which cuts across the composition in a slight diagonal line, was erected in 270 C. E. to protect the city from Germanic invaders. The height of the wall is suggested by the many small figures clustered around its base, and the structure's immense rectangular towers, constructed out of cut stone, are illuminated by the direct sunlight that washes over them.

Taking full advantage of his time abroad, Rosenberg also visited the ancient city of Constantinople (present day Istanbul) and, as might be expected, focused his attentions on the architectural wonders located there. He produced several etchings of the Byzantine church Hagia Sophia, which was built under the patronage of Justinian I. *The Great Bazaar, Constantinople*, also known as *The Grand Bazaar, Constantinople*, is a fine example of Rosenberg's facility with drypoint. In this masterfully rendered print the artist takes the viewer inside one of the world's most legendary marketplaces, for goods from every nation were once bought and sold in this congested city within a city. The stone vaulted interior is populated with different types of people who have come to examine the treasures to be found there. Although works like this attest to Rosenberg's skill with the etching needle, very little is known of his working methods. It is believed that all of the aforementioned etchings were based on preliminary sketches, which the artist later turned into etchings. Whereas many American etchers thought it necessary to print their own plates, Rosenberg was of a different mindset, and the firm of A. C. and H. W. Dickens Inc. in London served as his principal printer and agent.

Rosenberg's European adventures ended in 1927, and upon his return to the United States he settled in Fairfield, Connecticut; one of his neighbors was John Taylor Arms. The two etchers shared much in common, having etched many of the same subjects. A close professional friendship developed, with Arms and Rosenberg meeting regularly to exchange prints and criticisms. Rosenberg weathered the Great Depression with the aid of corporate commissions, and from 1928 to 1930 he worked on a series of twenty-two etchings documenting the construction of the Cleveland Railroad Terminal. These works were so successful that Rosenberg was hired two years later to create another suite of eight etchings that recorded the construction of another railroad terminal in Cincinnati.

When the market for prints began to decline in the early 1940s, Rosenberg laid aside his etching tools and turned his attentions once more to architectural work. From 1946 to 1964 the firm of York and Sawyer in New York City employed him, and upon his retirement he and his wife returned to Portland. Rosenberg spent the last years of his life compiling a journal that documented his travels and the etchings

Rue de Chartres, St. Malo,
(La Pomme d'Or) 1926
Etching and drypoint on laid paper
202 x 138 mm
8 x 5 1/2 inches
Spencer Museum of Art, The University of
Kansas: Bequest of Wallace Pratt, 1982.19

that resulted from them. In 1969 Rosenberg donated a large portion of his etchings and drypoints to the University of Oregon's Library of Special Collections, which maintains the largest collection of his work.

S O U R C E S :

Gail McMillan, *Catalogue of the Louis Conrad Rosenberg Collection* (Portland, Ore.: University of Oregon Special Collections Division, 1978).

Max Judge, "The Constantinople Etchings of L. C. Rosenberg," *The Print Collector's Quarterly* (July, 1928) 201-208.

Aurelian Wall, Rome, 1927
Etching on laid paper
211 x 301 mm
8 1/2 x 12 inches
Spencer Museum of Art, The University of
Kansas: 00.346

Rouen (Merry Christmas, Ernest & Elizabeth Roth), 1928
Etching on laid paper
154 x 84 mm
6 3/6 x 3 7/16 inches
Spencer Museum of Art, The University of Kansas: Gift in honor of Professor Stephen Goddard, 2003.101

Ernest David Roth

Born in Stuttgart, Germany, 1879
Died in Redding, Connecticut, 1964

Like many of the other artists in this exhibition Ernest David Roth possessed an insatiable wanderlust, demonstrated by his travels throughout Europe and North Africa. He explored Spain, France, Germany, Italy, Turkey, Tunisia, and Algeria, often retracing steps he had laid down years earlier. The etchings Roth created from these experiences reveal a sensibility remarkably attuned to the spirit of place. His portraits of places are unrivaled not only in their diversity and craftsmanship, but also in their ability to transport the viewer to other worlds.

Roth's family emigrated from Germany to the United States when he was approximately five years old; he became a New Yorker in early boyhood. As a youth he worked for an unknown art establishment by day, and in the evening studied etching at the National Academy of Design under James D. Smillie, a charter member of the New York Etching Club.

In the early 1900s Roth returned to Europe and made Florence, Italy his headquarters. He scoured his immediate environment for subjects worthy of etching, finding them in the picturesque neighborhood markets and bridge, such as Ponte Vecchio, which spans the Arno River. Like Monet, Roth was interested in the effects of sunlight on a particular object during different times of the day. The Ponte Vecchio became his favorite motif, and he created a remarkable series of etchings depicting it at various hours of the day and under different weather conditions. His acquaintances remember that Roth often disappeared for long periods of time to take etching expeditions to such distant locales as Toledo, Spain or Constantinople, and that he always returned with an interesting series of plates.

Whistler, who appears to have been his most influential teacher, heavily influenced Roth's etching technique. He employed Whistler's technique of biting the plate, applying the acid touch by touch with a feather, the blotting paper always close at hand. In the traditional process of multiple biting, three main values are generally produced, at most five. Employing Whistler's technique, Roth was able to attain as many as twelve values, which led to some adverse remarks from critics, one of whom described Roth as a painter etching, rather than a painter-etcher.[22]

[22] Frank Jewett Mather Jr. "The Etchings of Ernest D. Roth," *The Print Collectors' Quarterly* Vol. 1 (1911) 448.

He was known early on for his attention to detail, possessing a scrupulous respect for actual appearances, which he may have acquired from Smillie. While some critics applauded Roth's complex linear constructions, seeing in them evidence of his sincerity and individuality, others found them lacking in spontaneity and freedom of drawing, one of the most cherished tenets of the etching revival. In later works, like *Rouen*, Roth's drawing had become noticeably looser; the highly detailed realism of his earlier etchings had given way to abstraction and suggestion. As this work clearly shows, Roth had learned how to extract the most salient features of his subject, jotting down details with a mere flick of the needle. Beginning in the late 1910s and through the following decades, Roth produced a small etching every year based on his travels; these annual impressions were Christmas gifts for the closest friends and associates of Roth and his wife, Elizabeth. The Spencer's *Rouen* was mailed to supporters during the Christmas holidays in 1928. This impression came from the estate of Frederick Keppel, Roth's primary benefactor.

Roth created a series of etchings depicting New York City and its environs in the 1930s after his return to the United States, but there are few works that date after this time. Little is known of Roth's life and career after 1940. He settled in Redding, Connecticut and from all indications enjoyed a peaceful retirement.

SOURCES:

Frank Jewett Mather, Jr. "The Etchings of Ernest D. Roth," *Print Collectors' Quarterly* Vol. 1 (1911) 443-456.

Elizabeth Whitmore, *Ernest D. Roth, N. A. American Etchers, Vol. 1* (New York: The Crafton Collection Inc., 1929).

Carros, c. 1925
Etching and drypoint on wove paper
179 x 213 mm
7 1/16 x 8 5/8 inches
Spencer Museum of Art, The University of
Kansas: Anonymous Gift, 1998.588

JULES ANDRE SMITH

BORN IN HONG KONG, CHINA, 1880
DIED IN MAITLAND, FLORIDA, 1959

Throughout his long and varied career in the visual arts, Jules Andre Smith remained indifferent to either critical or public opinions of his work. He etched for the stimulation and satisfaction that his prints brought him, rather than to please others. A self-taught etcher, Smith took his lessons from numerous sources and he assimilated these disparate influences so thoroughly into his own evolving style that they are difficult to recognize. As his etchings demonstrate, Smith was an innovative and constantly probing artist. Not content to work in one manner for long, Smith in his prints documents the frequent radical changes in his art.

Like other etchers in this exhibition, Smith came to etching via a career in architecture. A graduate of Cornell College of Architecture, he spent less than a year working in an architect's office in New York before heading abroad in 1904; the journey was funded by a traveling fellowship he had received from Cornell. In Europe, Smith became interested in etching, which would become his chosen form of artistic expression for many years. Early etchings like *The Wood Road* (c. 1910), exhibit a tight drawing style and a literal adherence to factual information. In time, Smith's objective approach became decidedly more subjective and his lines more vibrant and idiosyncratic. He was less concerned with recording specific details, and sought instead to capture the truth of things, as he understood it.

Smith returned to the United States in the early 1910s and while he was working in the New York architectural firm of Dunbar and Ross he became acquainted with Ernest Roth. A warm friendship quickly developed between the two men that would last for many years. Around 1913 Smith and Roth began to take etching expeditions together and on at least one occasion they traveled to Europe, where they scoured the continent for worthwhile subjects. A comparison of their etchings from this time shows that they worked in a very similar style, which is characterized by a Whistlerian economy of means. Lines drawn upon the plate are clean and crisp, and there are large open areas in the compositions; the plates were often wiped clean. Perhaps the most obvious difference in their treatment of a particular subject is that Smith chose to include people in his prints, which teem with life, whereas Roth did not. The public spaces depicted in Smith's etchings are populated by a variety of people going about their daily business, as in *The Grim Towers of Loches*.

Smith and Roth parted company temporarily when World War I erupted in Europe. Roth passed the war years in the United States. Smith enlisted in the military in 1917 and, like his colleagues Kerr Eby and Lester Hornby, he served with the 40th Engineers Camouflage Unit. Smith was one of eight artists sent to the front to sketch the action, documenting the engagements at Belleau Woods, Château-Thierry, and St. Mihiel. One hundred of Smith's sketches were published in a book titled *In France with the American Expeditionary Forces* (New York: Hahlo, 1919). The informative drawings depict all aspects of the war, from the preparations for battle to its devastating conclusion.

With the war over, Smith and Roth returned to Europe in 1921. They traveled extensively in France and Spain, and it was during this journey abroad that their styles began to diverge markedly, as seen in Smith's *Grim Towers of Loches* and *Carros*, which date from the mid-1920s. As these etchings show, Smith's subjective approach was now firmly in place, for both prints are invested with a palpable sense of mystery. In Smith's *Grim Towers of Loches*, the city's famed medieval citadel is shrouded in meaningful darkness, its round pointed towers looming ominously above the cobblestone street lined with shops and homes. Built for the counts of Anjou in the mid-thirteenth century, the medieval structure served as a royal residence before being turned into a state prison. It was believed to have the deepest dungeons in the Loire Valley. The citadel's dark and oppressive history appears to be Smith's principal subject, as seen in its heavily shadowed façade, which is rendered in delicate cross-hatching; Smith's selective wiping of the plate further enhances the play of light and dark.

Smith's view of *Carros*, from about the same time, shows that his etching style was in a constant state of flux. A decidedly modernist influence can be seen here, for the twelfth-century château and surrounding landscape are rendered in geometric forms, which call to mind the late paintings of Paul Cézanne. Lines are straight and in some areas, such as the château, they lie parallel to one another much like the brushstrokes in Cézanne's canvases. Cross-hatching is used to define the dark brooding sky overhead as well as the shadows washing over the landscape below; contrasts of light and dark are accentuated by Smith's careful wiping of the plate.

Shortly after creating these etchings, Smith returned to the United States. While in basic training at Plattsburgh, New York in 1917 he had injured a leg, which never completely healed, and in 1925 the leg was amputated. Smith's travels to distant locales became increasingly difficult and came to an abrupt end in the late 1920s. From about 1930 on, most of Smith's etchings were devoted to religious subjects, like *The Man of Sorrows* (1930). Smith's eyesight began to fail in the early 1930s and by the middle of the decade he had turned away from etching in order to concentrate on other forms of artistic expression that required less scrutiny. The last twenty-five years of his life were devoted to painting, sculpture, and his efforts to construct an art school in Maitland, Florida. Smith's Research Studio opened in 1937. Conceived of as a workplace for painters and sculptors, it encouraged an experimental approach to art making. In the years since its opening the Research Studio has continued to attract many artists who have ascribed to Smith's belief that "An artist's job is to explore, to announce new visions, and open new doors."[23]

[23] Jules Andre Smith, qouted in Hall, 202.

Grim Towers of Loches, c. 1925
Etching on laid paper
250 x 182 mm
9 3/16 x 7 1/4 inches
Spencer Museum of Art, The University of
Kansas: Anonymous Gift, 1998.587

Sources:

Elton W. Hall, "The Etchings of Ernest Roth and Andre Smith," *Aspects of American Printmaking* (Syracuse, N.Y.: Syracuse University Press, 1988) 177-204.

J. Nilsen Laurvik, "Jules Andre Smith," *Print Collector's Quarterly* Vol. IV (1914) 167-82.

Grand Canal, Venice, 1905-10
Etching on laid paper
175 x 248 mm
6 3/4 x 9 3/4 inches
Anonymous Loan

Cadwallader Washburn

Born in Minneapolis, Minnesota, 1866
Died in Farmington, Maine, 1965

Having earned a Bachelor of Arts from Gallaudet University, the nation's preeminent institution of higher learning for the deaf, and a subsequent degree in architecture from the Massachusetts Institute of Technology, Cadwallader Washburn unexpectedly turned his attentions towards a career in the visual arts. In the early 1890s he attended the Art Students League, and there entered the orbit of William Merritt Chase. Christened the "silent artist" by his teacher and colleagues, he also spent several summers with Chase in Shinnecock, beginning in 1893. He eventually made his way to Paris and the studio of Albert Besnard, an accomplished etcher, and it was during their time together that Washburn laid aside his brushes in favor of the etcher's needle. His quick mastery of the medium proved advantageous, for in 1904 he was hired as a war correspondent for the *Chicago Daily News*, covering such conflicts as the Russian Japanese War (1904-05) and the Madera Revolution in Mexico (1910-12) in both words and images.

In pursuit of the picturesque, Washburn journeyed extensively throughout Europe, East Asia, and Central America. Like a host of other etchers, he answered Venice's beckoning call, arriving sometime after 1905; as this etching attests, he too fell under the spell of the magnificent palaces that appear to float mirage-like over the tranquil waters of the lagoon. The large structure to the left with striped awnings is the Palazzo Giustiniani Morosini. Constructed in 1474, the palace once served as the residence for one of the city's oldest and most powerful families, descendants of Venice's first patriarch Lorenzo Giustiniani (1386-1455), who was venerated for his asceticism and piety. To the right, separated by the Calle dei Tredici Martiri, is a less imposing building, known today as the Hotel Bauer Grunewald. Since Washburn's common practice was to draw directly on the plate, the actual location of the buildings is reversed in the print.

Although he was attracted to nature's essential elements, it was the first impression of a particular scene that Washburn sought to convey in his graphic work, and thus he simplified contrasts and eliminated superfluous details. In this work he calls the decaying buildings that line the Grand Canal into being with a few salient strokes of the etcher's needle, conveying a sense of their mass and substance with a purity and precision of line. Decorative elements such as balconies, railings, and awnings are rendered with lines of various widths and depths; the gondolier navigates his boat over the water in a flourish of swiftly laid lines. Doorways and windows are thrown into vivid relief by the suggestion of sunlight pouring over the building façades. While there is little information regarding Washburn's printing methods, one suspects from his writings on the subject that he also printed his own plates.

Deploring the crass commercialism to which etching had fallen prey at the close of the nineteenth century, Washburn exhibited little concern for the marketplace. In general, his small intimate works, beautifully drawn and judiciously bitten, preserve the intimate and personal characteristics of the medium, and discerning collectors eagerly snapped up his prints, which were issued in small editions. Although Washburn was drawn to architectural subjects for his etchings, he was also an exceptional portraitist. His subjects were generally people he encountered during his travels, and many of them have the appearance of elderly and wise sages.

S O U R C E S :
J. Nilsen Laurvik, *The Graphic Work of Cadwallader Washburn* (San Francisco: Hill Tolerton, The Print Rooms, 1916).

Cadwallader Washburn, "Notes of an Etcher in Mexico and Maine," *Print Collector's Quarterly* Vol. 1. no. 4 (1911) 64-81.

Above the Old Town, Amboise, c. 1920s
Etching on wove paper
325 x 231 mm
12 7/8 x 9 1/8 inches
Spencer Museum of Art, The University of
Kansas: Anonymous Gift, 1998.625

A. C. WEBB (ALONZO CHARLES)

BORN IN NASHVILLE, TENNESSEE, 1888
DIED IN RICHMOND, SURREY, ENGLAND, 1975

A. C. Webb believed that buildings possess a character that conveys the spirit of the people who constructed them, and for this reason he devoted his art to recording the architectural wonders of Europe and the United States. An architect by training, he possessed a deep admiration for the ancient buildings of Europe, which he feared would be destroyed by modern industry. He also displayed an appreciation for the skyscrapers that were quickly altering the the skylines of New York City and Chicago. Like a number of artists in this exhibition, Webb became an expatriate, returning to the United States only on special occasions.

One of twin boys born to Alonzo Charles Webb, a drawing teacher, and Ellen Hanor Webb, an amateur artist, he was given his father's name but disliked it so intensely that he preferred to be known by his initials, A. C. At the age of eighteen Webb moved to Chicago and enrolled at the Art Institute; he graduated three years later in 1909. He entered the University of Illinois at Champaign-Urbana in 1912, majoring in architectural engineering, but left two years later without completing his degree. Having absorbed the rudiments of a beaux-arts education, Webb made his way to New York City, where he studied under Kenneth Hayes Miller at the Art Students League from 1915-1916. Miller's lessons in representing the human figure appear to have had little impact on Webb, for people are noticeably absent from his artworks.

Webb enlisted in the Army when the United States entered World War I in 1917. He was sent to Calais, France with the Engineers of the 42nd (Rainbow) Division. He was transferred to heavy field artillery soon afterwards, and served as an instructor. Having fallen hopelessly in love with Paris during the war, Webb decided to make the French capital his home, and he resided there for nearly thirty years. Upon his discharge from the Army, Webb attended classes at the Allied Expeditionary Forces Training Center in Bellevue, just outside Paris, where he picked up his first etching needle. As Webb explained to a newspaper reporter in 1922, "I saw others doing etching and getting away with it, so I bought a copper plate, a needle, and a bottle of acid and went out and made me an etching."[24] He learned his craft by studying the works

24 A. C. Webb, cited in Susan Williams Knowles, *A. C. Webb: Artist/Architect* [MA Thesis] (Nashville, Tenn.: Vanderbilt University, 1986) 49.

of the masters, Meryon, Lalanne, and others. Taking advantage of the strong American dollar, which allowed him to live in Paris for very little money, Webb established a studio on the Rue du St. Gothard in Montparnasse and settled into printing etchings and drypoints; he produced at least sixty plates between 1920 and1929. Webb received many awards and honors during the 1920s. The French Government purchased his etching of Saint-Chapelle for the Musée de Luxembourg in 1922; for this work he was recognized in the press as one of the foremost etchers in France. While living in Paris in the 1920s, Webb spent six months of every year traveling the European continent and Northern Africa, taking in such exotic locales as Algiers, Tunis, and Morocco.

In 1929 Webb was invited by the Chicago Society of Etchers to serve on the jury of its annual exhibition. A respected member of the organization, he was also invited to create the 1929 annual print, which was mailed out to all of the members. His contribution, titled *Gothic Lace*, was issued in an edition of five hundred prints, all them bearing the blind stamp of the Society. In this evocative etching, which depicts one of the portals to Nôtre Dame de Paris, Webb displays his mastery of the medium by suggesting the way light washes over the intricately carved stonework, as well as the way it passes through the magnificent stained glass windows.

Webb's vantage point in *Above the Old Town, Amboise*, is the Château Amboise, which looms majestically above the quaint village. This palatial structure once belonged to the Counts of Anjou and Berry before the region came under French rule in 1434. The building was heavily damaged by one of Napoleon's politicians, Roger Duclos, who demolished two-thirds of it in the early nineteenth century; bombs dropped by the German Luftwaffe during World War II destroyed much of what was left. Today only a few features remain that preserve the original Renaissance charm of the structure: the façade facing the river, the Tour de Nîmes, and the Chapelle St. Hubert, which is believed to be the burial place of Leonardo da Vinci, who died in Clos Luce, a quarter of a mile away, in 1519.

When Webb returned to the United States briefly in 1929, his first visit since leaving for the war, he was struck by the radical changes that had been wrought in the New York skyline by the advent of the skyscraper. Captivated by their modernity and vertical power, Webb produced a large number of etchings, drawings, and water-colors depicting the skyscrapers then going up in Chicago and New York. In 1938 Webb and his wife Dorothy left their home in Paris and moved to the English coun-tryside; the threat of impending war in Europe was likely responsible for their deci-sion. They purchased Twyford Lodge, an Elizabethan manor house in the pictur-esque village of Richmond, Surrey, and settled into a comfortable semi-retirement.

S o u r c e s :
Susan Williams Knowles, *A. C. Webb: Artist/Architect* [MA Thesis] (Nashville, Tenn.: Vanderbilt University, 1986).

Gothic Lace, 1929
Etching on laid paper
246 x 160 mm
9 3/4 x 6 3/8 inches
Spencer Museum of Art, The University of
Kansas: Anonymous Gift, 1998.624

Spitalplatz, Strasburg, before 1914
Etching on laid paper
180 x 207 mm
7 1/4 x 8 1/4 inches
Spencer Museum of Art, The University of
Kansas: Anonymous Gift, 1998.627

Herman Armour Webster

Born in New York, New York, 1878
Died in New York, New York, 1970

While many etchers of his generation chose to follow Whistler's lead, Herman Webster was almost alone in taking his lessons from prints of the French master Charles Meryon. He first encountered Meryon's etchings by chance during a visit to the Bibliothèque Nationale in 1904. Moved by the mood and mystery of Meryon's plates, he resolved to make etching his métier. Like the poetic and romantic Meryon, he too sensed a living spirit in the old gray stones of the Parisian buildings. Conversely, the presence of modern life and the daily activities that animated the narrow alleyways and courtyards of Paris also fascinated Webster.

Webster's first visit to Paris was in 1900 following his graduation from Yale University; he studied art briefly with Alphonse Mucha (1860-1939). His family, which had already mapped out a business career for their son, voiced their disapproval and called him back to the United States. Around 1902 Webster took an extended trip to Asia, where he visited the great monuments of Japan and China. It was during this trip abroad that he recommitted himself to a career in the arts, and much to the chagrin of his family, returned to Paris, arriving in 1904. He enrolled in the Académie Julian and developed his drawing skills under Jean-Paul Laurens, Eugène Bejot and Félix Bracquemond, who may have provided him with the fundamentals of etching. However, Webster left after a year of formal instruction in order to devote more time to his study of Meryon's plates, as well as a number of instruction books on etching. Essentially self-taught, Webster received early encouragement and advice from his close friend Donald Shaw MacLaughlan, who was also living and working in Paris. They shared their knowledge and experiments, each of them developing an independent style well suited to his distinct personality.

Webster etched his first plate in the autumn of 1904 in Grez, a quaint village on the edge of the Fontainebleau forest. In the spring of 1905 he produced a small series of plates inspired by his trip to Spain, which included etchings of St. Martin's Bridge in Toledo, and the Mirada de la Reinas in the Alhambra. That same year, the Salon accepted four of his etchings. His reputation on the rise, he became a member of Royal Society of Painter-Etchers in 1907, and two years later, a member of the

Société des Peintre-gravures français. Additionally, Webster was the founder of the Société des Amis des Vieux Moulins, an organization for the preservation of old windmills, one of his favorite etching motifs. For his significant contributions to the artistic culture of the French state, Webster was made a chevalier of the Légion d'honneur in 1926, and in 1953 he was promoted to an officer.

An inveterate traveler, Webster was attracted to those relics of old-world architecture that are still to be found in places like Paris and Venice. Many of his etchings, like *Rue de la Parcheminerie*, are treasured because they record some nook or corner of a city that no longer exists. Although this street, located near the Seine on the left bank of, Paris, still remains, it has been completely transformed since Webster's time. In both this etching and *Spitalplatz, Strasburg*, Webster lavished special attention on the architectural details of the aged buildings that have seen so many generations come and go. Much like Meryon, he demonstrated a concern for the play of light and shadow. Webster also showed his mastery of representing human beings interacting in their environment; he was especially skilled in his placement of figures. With a few well-placed strokes of the needle he bestowed upon them a strong sense of character, for example the group of women talking in *Rue de la Parcheminerie* and the woman leading a child by the hand in *Spitalplatz, Strasburg*.

Webster's etched line is both disciplined and sensitive: He handles even the most profuse details with clarity and authority. He worked directly from his subject, once explaining to a critic, "I determine my composition in outline first. This outline I transfer to the plate. Then I go out and carefully study in pencil, on the original outline sketch, the subject I want to do, so as to to 'get acquainted' with it before beginning the more exacting work upon the copper-plate."[25] Webster also printed his etchings at his studio, which was located at No. 6 Rue Furstenberg, for he believed that only in his hands could the plate be made to yield all that it was meant to express. Webster also held that there was inherent beauty in the quality of the bitten line, and thus he avoided such special effects as plate tone.

[25] Webster, quoted in Hardie, p. 62.

When World War I erupted in 1914, Webster enlisted in the allied forces to defend his beloved France against German aggression. Unfortunately, his eyesight was so severely damaged by gas during one engagement that he was forced to lay down his etching needles for almost ten years. By the late 1920s, his eyesight had improved and he returned to etching the things he loved most, medieval cities, picturesque landscapes, and old windmills. Webster devoted a great amount of time to each of his plates and despite his slow and meticulous manner, he managed to produce more than 150 etchings during his career; Webster was still creating etchings of tranquil European landscapes well into his eighties without a noticeable loss of skill. Although he made Paris his home for nearly three-quarters of a century, Webster died in New York City.

S o u r c e s :

Martin Hardie, *Herman A. Webster* (New York: Frederick Keppel & Co., 1912).

Rue de la Parcheminerie, Paris, 1907
Etching on laid paper
277 x 176 mm
10 7/8 x 6 7/8 inches
Anonymous Loan

The Unsafe Tenement, 1858
Etching on laid paper
157 x 224 mm
6 3/16 x 8 7/8 inches
Spencer Museum of Art, The University of
Kansas: Gift of John J. Talleur and Ann
Talleur Collection, 1991.270

James Abbott McNeill Whistler

Born in Lowell, Massachusetts, 1834
Died in London, England, 1903

[26] Rensselaer, 15-16.

James Abbott McNeill Whistler's legacy as an artist rests significantly on his graphic work, specifically his etchings, which inspired a host of imitators and followers who looked to his prints as an example of the medium's possibilities. According to nineteenth-century art critic Mariana van Rensselaer, Whistler had "no superior among the moderns and few equals of any age."[26] Among Whistler's most important contributions, aside from the prints themselves, was his insistence on gesture, which is revealed not only in the idiosyncratic lines, but in the wiping of the plate. Whistler also devised a new compositional format known as the vignette that features a central focus, with elements becoming less distinct as one moves out from the center. He also insisted that the artist print his own plates, thus maintaining complete control over the entire process. As Deborah Johnson has explained, this last point is important, for it removed etching from the commercial production with which it had frequently been linked, and immediately improved etching's status in the fine arts. She adds, our modern definition of etching as a hand-wrought, hand-signed, limited edition work derives largely from Whistler's expansion of the medium.[27]

[27] Johnson, 10.

Whistler's beginnings as an artist and etcher of international importance can be found in the publication of a suite of etchings titled *Twelve Etchings after Nature*, more commonly known as the *French Set*, which was first published in 1858. Most of the plates that make up this set were created during a two-month journey along the Rhine, which Whistler undertook from August 14 to October 7, 1858. Whistler carried only ten copper plates with him on this expedition. A few of the etchings were based on preliminary drawings, a practice he would soon discard; the remaining images were sketched from nature, which would become his common practice. Among the best-known etchings of the series is *The Unsafe Tenement*. The rural subject matter, broken sketchy lines, and unworked areas found in this print suggest that Whistler was familiar with the etchings of Charles Jacque (1813-94), one of the most influential printmakers of the French etching revival.

In *The Unsafe Tenement* Whistler depicted a picturesque farmyard that could have been located anywhere in Northern France. The ramshackle structure occupying the center of the composition is bathed in direct sunlight, which enhances its meaningful details, such as the dog lying in the sun in front of the open doorway and the three-pronged pitchfork leaning against an exterior wall. Whistler's lines describe textures, and he used dense cross-hatching to create the dark shadows that lie under the roof line of the crumbling structure. Whistler's etching features a centralized focus, with areas around the perimeter of the building essentially left unworked; he would make extensive use of this format throughout his career.

In September 1879 Whistler undertook a long-delayed trip to Venice in order to complete a commission he had been awarded by the London Fine Arts Society for twelve etchings of the city, which were to be published in December of that year. The deadline passed, and Whistler remained in Venice for fourteen months, during which he produced fifty etchings and countless pastels of great beauty and delicacy. Whistler's Venetian etchings are the most important of his career and are considered to be one of the greatest achievements in the medium. Whistler published two series of etchings devoted to Venice. The first *Venice Set* was published under the aegis of the Fine Arts Society in 1880-81. The second *Venice Set*, comprised of twenty-six plates, was printed by Whistler and published by Dowdeswell & Dowdeswell in London in 1886-87. *The Garden* belongs to the second set and is one of Whistler's most remarkable etchings.

For *The Garden*, Whistler once again made use of the centralized motif, which had become a well-recognized feature of his prints by this time. He also employed a new compositional format, in which the viewer looks through a succession of framing devices, and which would be appropriated by many of his followers. Whistler likely sketched this scene from the vantage point of a gondola. The etching depicts a youth sitting on the water-washed steps leading down to a canal. His body language suggests that he has been caught in a daydream, and although he looks in the direction of the cat perched several steps above him, his thoughts lie elsewhere. The viewer is directed past the boy into a courtyard shaded by a large tree, and beyond to another doorway in which a woman and three small children are visible. One of the most remarkable details, and evidence of Whistler's virtuosity as an artist and etcher, is the reflection of the boy's leg in the murky waters of the canal. Whistler printed this rich impression of *The Garden*, believed to be from the eighth and final state, on old paper in brownish ink. He made extra impressions of this etching, which suggests the importance it had for him.

Whistler continued to produce etchings for the remainder of his career, but never surpassed the accomplishments he had achieved in Venice. His etchings became legendary during his lifetime and, as this exhibition demonstrates, greatly influenced succeeding generations of American etchers.

The Garden, 1880
Etching and drypoint on laid paper
305 x 238 mm
11 7/8 x 9 3/8 inches
Spencer Museum of Art, The University of
Kansas: Museum purchase, Helen Foresman
Spencer Art Acquisition Fund, 1990.3

S o u r c e s :

Deborah J. Johnson, *Whistler to Weidenaar, American prints 1870-1950* (Providence,
R.I.: Museum of Art, Rhode Island School of Design, 1987).

Katharine A. Lochnan, *The Etchings of James McNeill Whistler* (New Haven, Conn.:
Yale University Press, 1984).

Marian Griswold van Rensselaer, *American Etchers* (New York: Frederick Keppel &
Co., 1886).

GLOSSARY

aquatint

In the aquatint process, which is often employed with etched linework, the plate is first dusted with a powdery acid-resistant resin, then heated, which causes the grains of the resin to adhere to the plate. The plate is then bitten, resulting in a grainy surface that when printed, produces broad tonal passages.

biting

To "bite" a plate involves either immersing the plate in an acid bath or applying a mordant—depending on the material either nitric, sulfuric, or hydrochloric acid—directly on to the surface of the plate and moving it about with an improvised tool. The acid "eats" the exposed metal and produces a shallow, irregular line that holds the ink. Repeated bitings deepen lines; shallow lines can be protected from further biting or "stopped out" with a coat of acid-resistant varnish.

burin

The preferred tool of engravers, a burin is an instrument composed of a wooden handle and a steel shaft with a diamond-shaped point. The burin is pushed by hand along the surface of the plate and produces a clean, v-shaped line.

chine collé

"Chine" is an older term for very fine, tissue-like paper. In chine collé a sheet of this fine paper is laminated to a larger sheet of heavier paper at the time of printing.

drypoint

An intaglio process in which the needle scratches lines directly onto a plate that is not covered by a ground. There is no need for an acid bath since the drypoint needle produces a burr on one side of the line that holds ink and, when printed, produces a soft velvety line.

engraving

An intaglio process in which a burin is employed to create lines. Other techniques, such as etching, may be used in conjunction with engraving.

etching

An intaglio process in which the design is drawn through an acid-resistant ground with a needle exposing the metal surface underneath. The plate is then treated with a mordant or immersed in an acid bath, the acid "biting" the unprotected lines into the plate.

ground

An acid-resistant covering applied to the metal plate through which the needle is drawn. Recipes for the best ground have varied among etchers, but most have favored a mixture comprising wax, asphaltum, and pitch.

impression

An impression is an individual printing of the printmaking matrix (the metal plate, in the case of etching).

intaglio

Any of the techniques in which an image or tonal area is printed from lines or textures scratched or etched into a surface (usually a metal plate), such as engraving, etching, drypoint, aquatint, lift ground, or soft ground. The plate is covered with ink then wiped clean, leaving ink in the incised lines or textures of the image. This plate is then printed in a press on moistened paper. The paper is forced down into the area of the plate holding ink, and the image is transferred to the paper.

Japan paper

In traditional usage, any hand-made Asian paper might be described as "Japan." These papers are generally of very high quality and are similar to European laid papers, although the mould in which they are cast may be made of fine slats that have been wired together rather than purely of wire (see "laid paper").

laid paper

A hand-made paper that is cast in a paper mould. The mould is essentially a screen made of narrowly spaced wires held in place by widely spaced wires—somewhat like the cords that hold Venetian blinds together. The wires leave an impression in the paper when the paper is cast. The impressions of the widely-spaced wires are known as chain lines; the impressions of the narrowly spaced wires are called laid lines, hence "laid paper." See also "wove paper."

mezzotint

An intaglio process in which the artist works from dark to light. A tool with hundreds of fine teeth, known as a rocker, lays down a ground of very fine marks; the design is then burnished or scraped onto the plate, essentially erasing some of the marks laid down by the rocker.

monotype

A printing technique that produces a unique image rather than an edition of near-identical prints. The composition is drawn upon a plate with printer's ink or paint, then printed, either with a press or manually, by rubbing the back of the paper with the heel of the hand.

needle

A drawing instrument with an extremely sharp point, most generally used to create the lines in an etching. To draw lines, artists have used instruments such as old dental tools and sewing needles sharpened to a fine point.

plate tone

A film of ink laid down by the artist either during or after the wiping of the plate, which contributes tonal nuances to the printed image.

proof

A trial pull of a print, which allows the artist the opportunity to see whether any revisions must be made to the composition.

retroussage

A technique in which the etcher wipes the plate carefully in one direction (rather than with a circular motion), often with a stiff fabric called tarlatan. This careful wiping drags ink out of the etched lines. When printed, retroussage appears as a tonal shadow along each line.

soft-ground etching

An intaglio process in which the plate is first covered with a soft, waxy ground. A common use of soft-ground is the creation of pencil-like etched lines by laying a piece of paper on top of the soft-grounded plate. The artist then draws on the paper, which displaces the soft-ground on the plate. Many of the characteristics of pencil on paper are transferred through the ground, and when the plate is bitten these same characteristics appear when printed. Textures can also be applied to the plate by impressing different materials into the soft ground.

state

One of several distinguishable stages in the development of a print. Revisions are generally made between each state.

stopping out

Applying varnish or some other acid-resistant compound to etched lines, which protects them by preventing further biting.

wove paper

Paper, sometimes machine made, that is cast in a paper mould in which the wires of the mould screen (see "laid paper") are tightly woven like a window screen, hence "wove paper." Paper cast in such a mould shows relatively little texture from the screen.